YOUR MONEY LIFE: YOUR 50s

Peter Dunn

Cardiff Libraries
www.cardiff.gov.uk/libraries

Llyfrgelloedd Caerdydd
www.caerdydd.gov.uk/llyfrgelloedd

Cengage Learning PTR

Professional • Technical • Reference

Your Money Life:
Your 50s
Peter Dunn

Publisher and General Manager, Cengage Learning PTR:
Stacy L. Hiquet

Associate Director of Marketing:
Sarah Panella

Manager of Editorial Services:
Heather Talbot

Senior Product Manager:
Mitzi Koontz

Project Editor/Copy Editor:
Cathleen D. Small

Interior Layout Tech:
Bill Hartman

Indexer:
Sharon Shock

Proofreader:
Gene Redding

For product information and technology assistance, contact us at
Cengage Learning Customer & Sales Support, 1-800-354-9706

For permission to use material from this text or product,
submit all requests online at **cengage.com/permissions**
Further permissions questions can be emailed to
permissionrequest@cengage.com

Library of Congress Control Number: 2014954402

ISBN-13: 978-1-305-50793-7

ISBN-10: 1-305-50793-2

Cengage Learning PTR
20 Channel Center Street
Boston, MA 02210
USA

Cengage Learning is a leading provider of customized learning solutions with office locations around the globe, including Singapore, the United Kingdom, Australia, Mexico, Brazil, and Japan. Locate your local office at: **international.cengage.com/region**

Cengage Learning products are represented in Canada by Nelson Education, Ltd.

For your lifelong learning solutions, visit **cengageptr.com**

Visit our corporate website at **cengage.com**

Printed in the United States of America
1 2 3 4 5 6 7 16 15 14

This book is dedicated to you, the reader. The words in this book aren't about me or my family or anyone else who may have inspired me at some point in my life. This book is about you and Your Money Life. May the words impact and serve you.

ABOUT THE AUTHOR

Peter Dunn is an author, radio host, and personal finance expert who has developed content and curriculum for some of the world's largest financial companies. He was a financial advisor for nearly 15 years and managed several millions of dollars in assets. He is known for his down-to-earth and humorous approach that resonates with both consumers and financial industry insiders. He appears regularly on Fox News, Fox Business, and CNN Headline News, as well as several nationally syndicated radio programs. In 2012, Cision named him the fourth most influential personal finance broadcaster in the nation. Today, Peter's financial wellness firm develops financial wellness curricula for Fortune 500 companies.

Learn more at PeteThePlanner.com.

CONTENTS

Chapter 3: The Present: Spending   63

Chapter 4: The Pie: Budgeting 89

Chapter 5: The Possessions: Major Purchases 113

Chapter 6: The Picture: Income 147

Chapter 7: The Piggy Bank: Saving and Investing 179

Chapter 8: The Pitfalls: Insurance 207

Chapter 9: The Plan 233

Index 247

CHAPTER 1

THE PATH

The following statement may excite and/or terrify you: Your fifties should be the easiest decade of your financial life.

What do you feel right now? Excitement? Disbelief? Anger? No matter what you feel, I plan on making the case that you should, and can, exit your fifties with grace and financial ease. Don't get me wrong; there's still a ton of work to do, and you may still be in a transitional time from a parenting standpoint. But by the end of your fifties, you will begin to live your retirement lifestyle.

Notice my words there: I didn't say *you would be retired by age 60*. You might be, but that's not necessarily my goal for you. That's for you, your income, and your expenses to decide. I said that you will begin to *live your retirement lifestyle*. That's a big difference.

Allow me to paint the picture in very broad strokes.

Your fifties are your prime earning years. If your career trajectory has been relatively consistent, then cost-of-living adjustment raises, merit raises, and tenure and seniority pay increases have you earning more than ever before. I like that for you. Heck, you *love* that for you. But there's a bit of an issue: You are heading toward a period of time—let's call it retirement— that threatens to give you a permanent pay cut. So, if you're gliding toward a period of decreased income but all the while your income is increasing until you reach said period, how do you plan on throttling down appropriately?

You do need to throttle down—not your lifestyle or your level of activity necessarily, but your need for earned income. Retirement—or *financial independence*, as it's often called, although I believe *income independence* to be a more accurate moniker—is a period in which you trade in a paycheck derived directly from hours worked in the now to income streams derived from various other sources. Sure, you can work for your money in retirement. But a majority of your retirement income will likely come from non-work sources, such as a pension, Social Security, or your investments.

There's an underlying truth behind your transition from working to not working with regard to your investments. You will transition from the accumulation stage of your financial life to the distribution stage. Seems easy enough, right? Um, no. It's not exactly easy. Not only is it not easy, but your margin for error is slim in the distribution stage. Yet errors in distribution strategy don't appear for years after the errors are made. We'll dive deep into distribution strategy, but we've got a long row to hoe before then.

THE FREEDOM OF 50

I have had the great pleasure of observing thousands of financial lives. I've seen people transition through the decades of their financial lives. I've noticed something both surprising and invigorating: People love being in their fifties. Why?

At no period in your life will you have more disposable income, more assets, more time, and fewer children-related financial obligations (once your children finish school). Being in your fifties is like being a teenager again, but you have a heck of a lot more money. You may have already experienced this spirit of freedom, or you may sniff freedom drawing nigh. I'm glad you have this freedom, you're glad you have this freedom, and I know it feels great. But, there's a *but*.

Your freedom—the creation of slack in your financial rope—can backfire. I call this a *yo-yo retirement*. When fiftysomethings experience the great exhale that comes with financial freedom, complacency and newly formed financial habits fueled by an increase in discretionary funds can set in. And then when retirement arrives, a retightening—or an attempted retightening—occurs. Ladies and gentlemen, this is the yo-yo retirement. The initial exhale becomes the retirement you've always dreamed of, and retirement becomes difficult.

I like to think of the problem I just described as the rebirth of senioritis. Do you remember when you were a senior in high school or college, and that final-year apathy set in? That condition has been named senioritis. Simply put, it's apathy created by freedom. Growing retirement accounts, vanquished debts, and increased positive cash flow can summon senioritis. By the way, I'm sorry I called you a senior. Don't get too caught up in labels; they will just cause you grief. Although receiving your AARP card when you turned 50 was an uncomfortable moment, wasn't it?

So, how can you avoid cashing in your freedom chips too soon? How can you prevent this new form of senioritis? The easy answer is moderation. Moderation has always solved most consumption-related problems, hasn't it? The more nuanced answer in preventing senioritis revolves around living your retirement lifestyle now, permanently.

I know, I know, I know. I just told you that the problem is living your retirement lifestyle too early. Well, maybe that's what you thought you read. You didn't. I suggested that pre-retirees often go on a pre-retirement bender, which can significantly hinder their quest for retirement. My solution to the problem is to project retirement income streams, project retirement expenses, and then start trying to live on those parameters now. In an effort to do so, you will free up valuable income to pay down debt, save chunk money, increase retirement plan contributions, and most importantly, break your dependency on your work income. And just like that you've achieved income independence.

I suggested that you should be able to exit your fifties with ease. The reality is, you have to. How can you shut down your work income (retire) prior to knowing how to live on your retirement income? You can't. And you shouldn't. Whether you retire at 40, 55, 62, or 75, you must know what it's like to run your financial life on the income you will have available. If you haven't lived on the level of income you will have in retirement since you were 42 years old, you won't be able to make ends meet. You just won't. It's not an intelligence issue. It's not a math issue. It's a resources issue.

Dennis and Joanne were both 57 years old and had just finished paying for the third of their three children's college educations. What a relief this was! They were empty nesters, adjusting to the silence and enjoying it at the same time. With the elimination of bursar bills came increased discretionary income. This meant Dennis and Joanne were able to save more money for the future and improve their lifestyle significantly for the first time in more than 27 years, since they'd had children. They drove nicer cars, they ate better food, and they traveled. All of these expenses seemed as though they could be easily eliminated when necessary. Necessary being retirement, when income streams create lower income levels. But there was a tiny yet giant problem: Their new habits were, well, habit-forming.

Fast-forward nine years. Dennis and Joanne were now 66 and ready to retire. Dennis had a pension, they both planned to take Social Security retirement payments, and they were going to supplement those sources with distributions from their retirement investments. Despite the increased level of savings they created when their children left home for good, Dennis and Joanne had become desperately dependent on their new level of spending. Their lifestyle had expanded by the volume of their discretionary income increase when they were 57. They hadn't lived on the amount of money their retirement plan had ready for them in nearly 10 years. Not only that, but they hadn't budgeted, shown restraint, or even asked whether they could afford something once in the last 10 years.

THE TWIN ELEPHANTS IN THE ROOM

If you remove all the technical know-how, all the analysis, and all the math from the financial planning process of people in their fifties, you will find two questions. The first is, how much money do I need to retire? The second is, what's the proper mix of spending and enjoying money now and preparing for retirement? Both are very practical questions that deserve answers.

How much money do you need to retire? I get asked that question nearly every day of my life. In fact, on the day I wrote this section of the book, I was asked that question three times by 1 p.m. I'm going to try to answer the question for you, but you should know that only *you* can answer the question.

Do you remember Patrick Ewing? He was an NBA player from 1985 to 2002. I always point to him as the person who taught me the most about answering the "how much money do I need to retire" question. Huh? During the NBA lockout of 1998–99, Ewing, then president of the NBA Players Association, was trying to garner support for the players via the media. During one interview Ewing said, "We make a lot of money, but we spend a lot of money." And there you have it. What does it matter how much money you have, if you happen to spend all of it?

As you will read repeatedly in this book, if you aren't resourceful, then more resources won't really help you. The new resources will simply go the way of wasted resources. Anecdotally, I find that resourceful people need fewer retirement assets than they might think, and unresourceful people need more retirement assets than they think. I have found that, more than any other factor, your demand for assets, via your spending habits, will dictate your answer to the "how much money do I need" question.

You still want an answer, don't you? Okay, here's an answer. Read Chapter 6, "The Picture: Income." Although the question seems simple, it's not. There are too many factors to consider, such as other sources of retirement income, tax bracket, tax status of each retirement asset, and so on. But I will help you calculate the answer in Chapter 6, I promise. By the way, don't skip ahead.

The second elephant in the room addresses the proper mix of spending money and enjoying life now versus sacrificing now to prepare for retirement. This question is best answered by a question. If you keep doing what you're doing, given your current asset levels, spending habits, and monthly investment deposits, is your retirement looking good? If yes, feel free to keep on keepin' on, and spend your excess money however you want on whatever you want. If no, then…don't. If your retirement isn't secured by your past actions and your current habits, then you must not only show some consumer restraint, but also buck up and start fixing your problem. Good news, though— this book can help you do that.

All right. We've recognized the lovely twin elephants in the room. Now we must recognize a few other small pachyderms.

FINANCIAL SUPPORT OF ADULT CHILDREN

Prepare yourself for some discomfort. Without a doubt, one of the most damaging things you can do as you approach retirement is to financially support your adult children in any way. Experts have called this phenomenon "failure to launch." Your inability to separate yourself from your adult child is a failure. That's what makes this situation difficult. The assertion seems both callous and unreasonable, yet cultural trends suggest that this is a significant problem in our society.

Take a look at the raw data from a 2011 National Endowment for Financial Education report.

▶ 50 percent of parents supply housing to adult children who are no longer in school.

▶ 48 percent of parents supply money for living expenses to adult children who are no longer in school.

▶ 41 percent of parents assist with transportation costs for adult children who are no longer in school.

▶ 35 percent of parents provide insurance coverage for adult children who are no longer in school.

▶ 29 percent of parents occasionally front spending money for adult children who are no longer in school.

▶ 28 percent of parents pay medical bills for adult children who are no longer in school.

These numbers are ridiculous. Your kids have training wheels on. Can you imagine the Tour de France if the cyclists rode with training wheels? The Tour de France is one of the most difficult athletic competitions in the world. It is very dangerous, it takes years of dedication and hard work to prepare for, and it wouldn't be possible if the athletes' parents didn't let their children fall off their bikes.

When children learn to ride a bike, they inevitably fall. A fall from a bike is usually followed by a little bit of pain and some tears. Sometimes the fall is followed by more than a little bit of pain and some tears. As a parent, it's quite difficult to watch your child not only fail, but also be in pain. Does it make you a bad parent if your daughter falls off her bike and bloodies her knee? Absolutely not, and yet it does take a large amount of internal fortitude.

Your children need to fall off their financial bikes. They need to fail financially. It doesn't make you a bad parent if you allow your children to fail financially; it makes you a bad parent if you take away their opportunity to learn. Did they rack up a large amount of credit card debt, making it tough for them to handle their bills? It sounds like the perfect chance to learn a lesson.

However, here's the very difficult part: Your children's financial mistakes can often be attributed to you not teaching them the proper way to handle money. No one wants to read this, especially if you have been in this situation in the past. If you have found yourself in this situation, you have to ask yourself a series of probing questions. What did you fail to teach your children about money? How can them solving their own problems help them learn? Did your financial assistance treat the problem, the symptoms, or the side effects?

If you have already driven down this road of financial assistance and haven't been able to sever financial ties, then you need to do so before this relationship ruins your retirement. Don't think it can't actually ruin—and not just damage—your retirement. It can absolutely ruin it. You only have so many working years left; your child has many more working years remaining.

One of the most common manifestations of failure to launch is when a parent loans/gifts a child a down payment to purchase a home. The scenario usually goes like this: The child can afford the mortgage payment but can't qualify for the mortgage loan unless he or she has money for a down payment. The parent offers to step in and loan/gift the money for the down payment. The mortgage application is approved, and chaos ensues.

What? You didn't know about the chaos part of this scenario? Let's examine the scenario from a different perspective: Why did the lending institution require a down payment? Because it's a significant measure of whether someone is a good credit risk. What did you do to the process? You destroyed it—not only for the lending institution, but also for your child. You helped your child get into a 30-year mortgage agreement he or she couldn't afford. Affording a home is more than just affording the payment. What's going to happen when the house needs a new furnace? What's going to happen if the street your child lives on needs a sewer upgrade, and the homeowners on the street are responsible for paying for it? What are you going to do if your child loses his or her job?

Good parenting is helping your child avoid these situations, rather than facilitating them. Good parenting is letting your child get denied the loan, then showing him or her how to save the money for the down payment. Bad parenting is solving a problem that didn't exist and creating a problem that didn't exist.

When people ask for help, they generally look for help from someone in a better financial position. When they need a rescue lifesaver in the water, they usually look for someone who isn't in the water. When someone knocks on your door wanting to borrow a cup of sugar, he or she is simply looking for someone who has more sugar. In other words, all of these people are looking for help from someone with a relative advantage.

Just because you have more money or a higher income than another person, that doesn't mean you are in a position to help that person. Human nature and parental instinct would tell you otherwise. Your unwillingness to help someone can be interpreted as cruel and selfish, but it's neither. What's cruel is helping someone when you shouldn't, especially if it means hurting yourself in the process. When given preflight instructions on a commercial aircraft, passengers are told that in the case of an emergency, they should secure their own oxygen masks prior to assisting the person next to them. Why? Because you risk everyone's safety when you can't ensure your own safety.

YOUR PARENTS

You know that you're responsible for your financial life, you've promised to cut the cord to your children when appropriate (right?), but there's one more entity that may require your money's attention: your parents.

If your parents aren't properly prepared for financial life as aging Americans, then you may be compelled to step in and facilitate their comfort. I'm not here to suggest that your assistance is good, bad, or otherwise. But no matter what assistance strategy you choose, just know that it will likely have a financial impact on your life. Dropping everything to help people in their time of need has its consequences. Understanding those consequences—and better yet, finding ways to prevent the events and mitigate the consequences—is not only possible, but advisable.

As you'll learn when we discuss your own need for long-term care insurance in Chapter 8, "The Pitfalls: Insurance," there are ways to prevent your family from feeling the financial burdens that can come with a lack of preparedness.

It is vital for you to have a discussion with your parents about their financial lives. You need to understand their assets, their debts, their insurance coverage, and their estate plan (will and/or trust). Not only that, but based on how they age, you may need to take legal control of their assets and decision-making. While it's certainly not fun to think about, it's a lot less fun to actually do. The sooner you can have conversations, the sooner you can help them prepare for what lies ahead. As you can imagine, your discussions with them aren't in an effort to preserve whatever estate you might inherit; instead, the discussions are to make sure they have enough money to last them throughout their lives.

Once you're able to delicately deal with the generations sandwiched around you, your full focus can turn toward securing your financial life forever.

WHAT YOU WILL LEARN IN THIS BOOK

Your Money Life: Your 50s has eight more chapters after this one. Each chapter is dedicated to helping you understand everything you need to know about very important financial topics.

DEBT

Your attitude toward debt is a direct product of your upbringing. You need to understand how to properly leverage debt and how to avoid thinking you are properly leveraging debt when in reality you aren't. Debt isn't evil, but a casual attitude toward debt can render your financial life miserable.

You'll learn how debt can negatively impact your retirement and what to do about it.

SPENDING

Control your spending, and you will be able to control your financial life. If you don't have control over your spending, you'll never make enough money to fund your lifestyle. One of the end goals of financial wellness is resourcefulness.

As you will learn, it's okay to occasionally splurge and buy something you normally wouldn't buy. In fact, learning when to splurge and when not to splurge will help you keep your financial stress in check. You've heard a thousand times why you should watch how much you dine out and spend on utilities, but this time I'm going to show you exactly how to do it while still living a normal life. We'll discuss when moderation is best and when it's best thrown out the window.

BUDGETING

You can't earn your way out of the need to budget. You can't make so much money that decision-making becomes unimportant. In retirement, you will have a finite amount of assets and income. Budgeting makes it possible for these resources to be enough, no matter how much you start with.

MAJOR PURCHASES

The success of your financial life is largely determined by your ability to make wise spending decisions about both big and small items. Budgeting will help you address the small decisions, but you'll need a comprehensive major-purchase strategy to stay out of big trouble. Your car and home purchases are tricky, given lenders' willingness to put you in an objectively rough financial situation.

You will learn exactly how much house and car you can afford and how they impact your ability to retire.

INCOME

You've heard the term *financial independence* a million times. What is it and what does it mean? It means you aren't dependent on work income. Well, if you aren't dependent on work income, then you must be dependent on some sort of income, right? You are. Your retirement income sources allow you to not work. You will learn how these income sources work and how they will support you in your effort to have a successful and comfortable retirement.

Additionally, you will lean the importance of Monte Carlo simulations and distribution rates.

SAVING AND INVESTING

You need to know how your assets work. Whether your retirement accounts are annuities, 401(k)s, CDs, or stocks, you need to understand exactly how those vehicles will affect your retirement planning. You will learn about risk, time horizon, and how to deal with your financial advisor.

INSURANCE

Your fifties is an interesting time from an insurance perspective because of the overlap. You will be buying some new coverage, dropping some old coverage, and in some cases finding yourself with more insurance premiums than ever before.

A PLAN

Life will throw you all sorts of financial curveballs. But if you have a plan, you will be prepared not only for the good times, but also for the bad times. You will have a step-by-step action plan for what to do next. If you are motivated to better your financial life, I've got good news for you: Your motivation plus an action plan will equal financial progress. And that's why you got this book, right?

YOUR REMOVABLE GUIDE

While it would be great if you could walk around with this book all the time; it's not exactly practical or realistic. What is realistic, though, is giving you a functional, focused, and powerful guide to keep track of your goals, progress, and information. Enter the *Your Money Life* guide.

A budget is worthless if you never look at it. Your financial goals are pointless if you never measure your progress toward them. And the power of your net worth goes untapped if you don't track it. The *Your Money Life* guide allows you to do all of these things in one convenient location.

GET STARTED

Your ability to juggle money to tend to your past, present, and future will determine your financial success. We're constantly told to live in the now and to plan for the future. But to do that, we must address our past. So regardless of whether it stresses you out, it's time to open the door to your past financial decisions and explore your debts.

CHAPTER 2

THE PAST: DEBT

On the surface, debt seems like it's only an issue for young families. There's the family home, the family cars, the vacations, the educations, and several other expenses debt seems justified to be a part of. But what happens when the kids move out? What happens when the last family vacation is taken and the last diploma is earned? Unfortunately, in today's America, the empty nesters who so badly want to focus on their relationship again are often left saddled with copious amounts of debt of every possible variety.

The average American household had roughly $7,000 in consumer debt in 2013. But when you remove the households that have zero consumer debt, something interesting happens. The average household with *any* consumer debt has more than $15,000 in consumer debt.

Debt levels in the United States have grown at a ridiculous pace as more and more consumers have decided that they want to play the debt game. In 1943, there was more than $6.5 billion in outstanding consumer credit. As of June 2014, there is $3.2 trillion of outstanding consumer credit.[1] And while I'm sure some of the $3.2 trillion worth of consumer debt is at 0 percent interest, the vast majority of that debt costs borrowers a significant amount of money. You can't forget that when you borrow, the interest rate you pay makes the item(s) you are purchasing more expensive. A $20,000 car will cost you $21,675.89 when you finance it for 48 months with a 4 percent interest rate. That's 8.4 percent more than you have to pay.

---

[1] http://www.federalreserve.gov/releases/g19/hist/ cc_hist_sa_levels.html.

People in their fifties often face mortgage debt, credit card debt, parent student loans, and various other forms of consumer debt. According to a 2013 Census Bureau study, mortgage debt accounts for 78 percent of all household debt in America. And in the 55-to-64 age category, Americans carry on average $70,000 in debt, which is a 64 percent increase since the year 2000. The numbers further suggest the average pre-retiree is dealing with nearly $55,000 in mortgage debt and $15,000 in other consumer debt. These totals will make for an uncomfortable and difficult retirement if not dealt with appropriately.

TYPES OF DEBT

There are several different types of debt, and many of them have unique characteristics. It's imperative that you know how each type of debt works, the truths surrounding the debts, and where the type of debt falls on the Good Debt/Bad Debt scale.

The Good Debt/Bad Debt scale is an admittedly subjective scale on which you can begin to measure the utility of each different type of debt. A 1 on the Good Debt/Bad Debt scale indicates that there is close to zero sense in having or holding that type of debt. A 5 on the scale indicates that you're properly leveraging debt to improve your overall financial standing. I'm not going to go so far as to say there are good debts. But I will admit some debts are relatively better to hold than others.

For instance, I think a mortgage is the best debt to have, on a relative basis. But I'd rather you not have a mortgage at all.

I don't really care about deducting the mortgage interest on your taxes. If you didn't have a mortgage payment, then your cash flow would still net positive compared to having a mortgage payment and deducting the mortgage interest on your taxes.

Consider this: If your gross household income is $80,000 and you pay $5,000 in mortgage interest, then your taxable income will become $75,000, after you've claimed the mortgage-interest deduction on your tax return. Now, let's say you have a marginal tax rate of 25 percent. Your mortgage-interest deduction just saved you $1,250 in taxes. I've got to admit, that's pretty awesome. You paid $5,000 in interest and reduced your taxes by $1,250, for a net outflow of $3,750. Let's now consider the alternative.

If you don't have any mortgage interest to deduct, your taxable income will remain $80,000. You don't get to legally avoid $1,250 in taxes, but you also don't have to pay $5,000 in mortgage interest. Whereas having mortgage interest to deduct (in our previous example) results in a net cash outflow of $3,750, having no mortgage interest to deduct results in a net cash outflow of $0. The choice is simple. If you keep a mortgage so that you can deduct the interest, you will pay a net amount of $3,750. If you don't have a mortgage, you will pay nothing.

The "keeping a mortgage to deduct the interest expense" myth is another example of trying to out-math math.

We will discuss the proper way to pay off your debts later in this chapter, but you should feel especially compelled to pay off your debts that fall on the low end of the Good Debt/Bad Debt scale. That being said, don't be dismissive of the debts you have on the top end of the Good Debt/Bad Debt scale.

STUDENT LOANS

Based on new statistics, it's quite possible that you still have some student loan debt hanging around. At this point in your life, you can't afford to be financially tied to your education, especially if it took place late in your career. The money you are paying toward your student loans is needed for your other financial priorities, including retirement.

While student loans certainly don't have some of the nasty interest rates that can come with credit card debt, the monthly obligation is something you need to eliminate.

Good Debt/Bad Debt rating: 2

Analysis: Just because you're in your fifties doesn't mean that you're necessarily done with student loan debt forever, although arguably you probably should be. The changing nature of education and retirement has led to some unexpected side effects.

The reality is that more seniors than ever before are dealing with student loan debt. According to a report from the United States Government Accountability Office, between 2005 and 2013, student loan debt among seniors 65 and older rose by more than 600 percent, from $2.8 billion to $18 billion. And it's not just student loan debt that was acquired to educate the children of this demographic. Eighty percent of this $18 billion in student loan debt is for the borrower's education, not their children's.

Enlightenment, whether you like it or not, comes at a price. While a career change late in the game is both inspiring and riveting, it also has serious financial ramifications that can affect retirement cash flow for the rest of your life.

Student Loan Intricacies

Of course, the other element here is the fact that you might be helping your children fund their educations. We'll look at your direct help in a moment, in the "Parent Student Loans" section, but you also need to look at how your children might be saddled with student loan debt.

Below, you will see the major differences between federal and private student loans. As you help your children make the best decisions for their education, don't forget the long-lasting financial implications.

Federal (subsidized) student loans

- Your children don't need a credit check to obtain federal student loans. Yet these loans can help your children establish healthy credit.

- The nature of a subsidized loan is that the government will pay the interest payments on the loan for students with financial needs while the borrower is still at least a half-time student.

- Your children don't need you to cosign on federal loans.

- Your children don't have to start repaying their federal loans until they are no longer classified as a student (they graduate, leave school, or switch to being less than a half-time student).

- Interest rates are fixed and are generally lower than the rates on private student loans.

Private student loans

- No one pays the interest on private student loans but the student. There are no interest subsidies.
- Interest rates are variable and can approach 20 percent.
- Many private student loans require your child to start making payments while he or she is still in school.
- Your children have to qualify for private loans via their credit score or a cosigner (you).

While many student-loan programs will allow students 25 years to repay their debts, they shouldn't take this long. Ten years is the standard loan-repayment period for a reason. Your children should get their education and then pay it off. They shouldn't live with student-loan debt for a quarter century just because they are allowed to.

PARENT STUDENT LOANS

Feel free to skip this section if you won't be in the position to have a college age student. Better yet, don't skip it. You are about to learn about one of the biggest problems effecting retirement planning today.

Seventy-one percent of college seniors who graduated in 2013 had student loans. The average balance of the student loans was roughly $30,000. Student loans are available either through the federal government or through your university/college, bank, or credit union, usually as part of a financial-aid package.

Student loans are among the most substantial types of debt for recent college graduates, and they are becoming more common for parents, too. According to a study cited in *The Wall Street Journal*, over the last decade the average student-loan debt in the United States has increased significantly—from roughly $18,000 in 2004 to $33,000 in 2014. The percentage of students graduating with debt has also risen from 64 percent in 2004 to 71 percent in 2014.[2]

Parent student loans—or Parent PLUS Loans, as they're often called—are loans that parents take out for their children's college education. When a student begins the matriculation process—and yes, I just wanted to use the word *matriculation*—families often turn to the Free Application For Student Aid (FAFSA) to seek financial aid. The FAFSA helps determines what a family's Expected Family Contribution (EFC) is. The EFC determines how much financial aid a family receives. I know, lots of acronyms and lots of confusion. But simply put, it works like this: A college provides a family a Cost Of Attendance (COA) number, the FAFSA determines the family's EFC, and then the COA minus the EFC determines a family's eligibility for need-based aid. Okay, fine, it's not simple.

Need-based aid includes programs such as Pell Grants, Perkins Loans, and direct student loans (borrowed by students). What if a family doesn't get enough need-based aid? Enter programs such as Parent PLUS Loans. If a family has a solid household income, reasonable assets, and not a tremendous number of college age children, they won't get the amount of need-based aid they might desire.

---

[2] http://blogs.wsj.com/numbers/congatulations-to-class-of-2014-the-most-indebted-ever-1368.

Good Debt/Bad Debt rating: 2

Analysis: It is not my intent to be controversial in giving parent student loans a 2 on the Good Debt/Bad Debt rating scale. My intent is to help you understand the impact Parent PLUS Loans can have on *your* financial life. Whether you choose to pay for your children's education is your decision to make. Just know that there are many better ways to accomplish your goal than borrowing to pay for your kids' education. We'll discuss those strategies later in the book.

Default rates on Parent PLUS Loans have skyrocketed.[3] In 2006, 1.8 percent of Parent PLUS borrowers were in default. By 2010, default rates had nearly tripled to 5.1 percent. Tripled! And this on the heels of tougher requirements. The increased scrutiny on parents' credit scores has saved many parents from being potential default cases as well.

BANK CREDIT CARD DEBT

Consumer credit tools can be traced back to the 1800s, when oil companies and general merchants extended credit to their individual consumers. It wasn't until the 1960s that a national system for accepting credit cards was implemented. The companies we now know as MasterCard and Visa were among the trailblazers of the consumer credit industry.

Credit cards are more prevalent today than ever before. This increased usage has led to a treasure trove of problems. High

---

[3] https://www.insidehighered.com/news/2014/04/03/education-department-releases-default-data-controversial-parent-plus-loans.

interest rates, penalties, and fees associated with your credit cards can quickly add up. It's much more important to focus on your financial health, not some arbitrary score that can take you down a nasty path. In fact, your credit score, that mystical metric that is often pointed to as the bastion of financial wellness, isn't a very good indicator of your financial health. Net worth, which is your assets minus your liabilities, paints a much clearer picture. Wouldn't you rather reduce your debts and increase your savings than manipulate an overrated number that just proves you are good at borrowing?

You'll notice that our discussion on credit cards will continue throughout this book. This is purposeful, the opposite of subtle, and the biggest hint you have ever been given.

Good Debt/Bad Debt rating: 1

Analysis: Why? Why do it? You don't need to. Save money, and then use the money to buy stuff you want. Don't borrow and then find a way to pay for it later. When you do that, you will end up paying more for your purchases. And for you "pay off your credit card at the end of each month" people, I've got a little something for you later in the book.

STORE CREDIT CARD DEBT

Nearly every major retailer—from Gap to Amazon to Walmart—offers customers the opportunity to apply for a credit card that can be used only in their store. They lure customers into signing up for their cards with an interest-free grace period (usually the first six months) or a discount on their purchases.

Consumers get into trouble when they neglect to pay off their balances—or when they use their cards beyond the interest-free grace period. Store credit cards offer high interest rates, many of them right around 25 percent. It doesn't take long for an interest rate that high to wreak havoc on someone's financial health. In addition, they do little to impact your credit score, and they have low limits, putting you at risk for added fees.

Store credit cards exist for one simple reason: to sell you more stuff. Every deal, coupon, or special offer is designed to induce spending, not help you. Store credit programs are created under the guise of loyalty programs, but who is being loyal to whom? In nearly every extreme debt situation I have ever encountered, store credit cards are present. They are a financial gateway drug.

Your best bet is to avoid store credit cards altogether. Signing up for a card to defer payment for an item over six months is a good indication that you shouldn't be buying that item in the first place.

Good Debt/Bad Debt rating: 1

Analysis: Store credit cards are as unnecessary as they are dangerous. They aren't collector cards. If your wallet has space for six credit cards, buy a smaller wallet. Don't fill up the wallet with store credit cards. Oh, and don't buy the wallet using a credit card.

CAR LOAN

Unless you live in the heart of a major city and have access to safe and affordable mass transit, chances are you're going to have to buy a car. While a car is arguably a necessity in the twenty-first century, it doesn't mean you have to disregard sensibility and contribute to the growing trend of skyrocketing car loans.

According to Experian Automotive, which tracks millions of auto loans written each quarter, the average amount borrowed by new car buyers in the fourth quarter of 2013 was a record-high $27,430. The average monthly payment for a new car was $471, and the average monthly payment for a used-car loan was $352.[4]

To make matters even worse, a record 20 percent of new-car loans were extended beyond six years. A car is one of the worst investments you can make. It depreciates in value immediately after you drive it off the lot and continues to depreciate for the duration of the time you own it. Borrowing money to buy a depreciating asset isn't a great idea. By the mere fact that there is an interest charge associated with the loan, you are paying more for a car than it's worth, and when you have paid it off, it's worth even less.

Good Debt/Bad Debt rating: 3

Analysis: It's not the end of the world if you have car debt, but it's also not the best idea. If you ever find yourself underwater on a car (meaning you owe more on the car than it's worth), don't trade in the car and finance the entire process. You will

---

[4] http://www.cnbc.com/id/101461972#.

drive off the lot owing more on your new car than it's worth, and your new car will instantly depreciate even further when you take it off the lot. Again, just because a car dealer will let you borrow $40,000 on a $30,000 car doesn't mean you should do it.

HOME LOAN (MORTGAGE)

As you will learn in Chapter 5, "The Possessions: Major Purchases," the type of mortgage you have is incredibly important. A mortgage can be a decent use of debt because the underlying asset (the house) is, generally speaking, an appreciating asset. An appreciating asset is an asset that goes up in value over time. So by the time you have paid off your mortgage, the home itself generally, but not always, will have increased in value.

Good Debt/Bad Debt rating: 5

Analysis: A home is an asset that is easily exchanged in a reasonable marketplace. You don't necessarily have to wait until the end of your mortgage term to profit on the buying and selling of a house. Of any debt you could ever possibly acquire, this is the best one. But remember, we're comparing a mortgage to the likes of credit cards and payday loans.

Carrying a mortgage deep into retirement puts a tremendous amount of pressure on your retirement income sources. If you are fearful you won't have enough money to retire, then make a concerted effort to pay off your biggest retirement expense, such as your mortgage, thus eliminating the need for a copious amount of retirement income.

MEDICAL DEBT

Rising medical costs and insurance premiums have made medical debt the number-one cause of bankruptcy filings in the United States, according to a recent study from NerdWallet Health. More than 1.7 million Americans will file bankruptcy because of unpaid medical bills in the next year, and 56 million adults—more than 20 percent of the population between 19 and 64—will struggle with medical debt. In an attempt to pay off their debt, more than 11 million people will increase their credit card debt as well.

While preparing for medical debt can be difficult—especially as a young person at the peak of his or her physical health—building up a significant emergency savings fund and funding a Health Savings Account (HSA), when applicable, can help offset the financial repercussions of medical expenses.

Anecdotally, medical debt has always seemed to me to be the most ignored. I've witnessed a great number of people exhibit outright dismissive attitudes about medical debt. You'll learn more about how to protect yourself from medical debt in Chapter 8, "The Pitfalls: Insurance."

Good Debt/Bad Debt rating: 4

Analysis: While you shouldn't carry medical debt, if you happen to acquire some due to medical issues, you shouldn't panic. Your health is very important, and if you make wise health-care decisions, you can feel justified in spending money on improving your health. Medical debt tends to bring quite a bit of stress, because of the residual stress associated with the root medical problem. Do not interpret a rating of 4 on the Good Debt/Bad Debt scale as justification to ignore your medical debts. However, if there is a debt about which you truly don't have a choice, it's medical debt. Take it seriously.

LINES OF CREDIT (SECURED AND UNSECURED)

A line of credit is different from a loan in that it's not one lump sum of money. Instead, you can draw from a specified amount of money in your line of credit in the same way that you would use a credit card. There are two types of lines of credit: secured and unsecured.

A secured line of credit is one that is backed by collateral, such as a house or another piece of property. An unsecured line of credit is one that has no collateral backing it up. Because unsecured lines of credit are riskier for lenders, their interest rates are significantly higher than secured lines of credit.

Both are risky for borrowers, and for different reasons. If you can't pay back your secured line of credit, you put yourself at risk of losing whatever collateral you've offered up. If you can't pay back your unsecured line of credit, high interest rates can add up quickly. Be very careful when tapping a line of credit, which can certainly have a blank-check quality to it.

It's not uncommon for homeowners to tap their equity line of credit to make home improvements. Sometimes the home improvements increase the underlying property value, and sometimes they don't. You've heard it a million times, and in case you haven't, let me say it again: Your house is not a piggy bank. Removing equity from your home, even to theoretically increase the value of your home via home-improvement projects, is a bad idea. Home-improvement projects very rarely equal a dollar-for-dollar increase in home value. That $15,000 landscaping job you just completed probably did close to nothing for the value of your home.

Good Debt/Bad Debt rating: 2

Analysis: If you own a home, you will be presented with the opportunity to rob your home of its equity. Sure, it's called a home equity line of credit (HELOC), and it sounds innocuous. But it's not. It doesn't make sense to borrow against an asset you've already established. Use your income to push your financial life forward. Don't tap the assets you've already worked so hard to build. When you take out a line of credit, you will run in place financially.

REVERSE MORTGAGE

You aren't old enough to participate in the reverse mortgage process, but you should still understand how they work. Your parents are likely the target market for many of the advertisements associated with reverse mortgages. Additionally, if you had planned on using a reverse mortgage as part of your retirement strategy, then you should understand the ramifications of getting one.

It's hard to turn on the TV or pick up your favorite magazine and not see an ad for reverse mortgages. If you know anything at all about the idea of a reverse mortgage, you instantly understand their appeal. Simply put, all the payments you made to the bank in an effort to own your home outright can be reversed back out to you. In a reverse mortgage, the bank starts paying you your equity, and you still get to live in your house. Seems great, right?

Well, it's not that simple. Of course it's not that simple. I'm pretty sure you've learned at this point in your life that financial tools are never as simple as they may seem. A reverse mortgage is in fact a debt. It is a debt that must be paid—either by your estate at your passing or by you, when you may not be in a position to pay back a giant chunk of money.

When you are 62 years old or older and you own your home outright, a reverse mortgage is a possibility. The million-dollar question is whether it's a good idea.

Reverse mortgages make my top-three list of most complicated financial products (along with variable annuities and index annuities). To be fair, their complicated nature doesn't make them bad. When I think about complicated financial products, I often think about how the benefits are presented in the sales process early, but the disadvantages can be glossed over or altogether dismissed due to the technical complexities that are present.

Let's examine some distilled pros and cons of using a reverse mortgage.

Pros

▶ A reverse mortgage unlocks and distributes the equity in your primary residence when you need a lump sum of money or a regular income stream.

▶ Reverse mortgage debts generally don't need to be repaid until the borrower's death. The debt needs to be paid when you die, when you sell your home, or when the home is no longer considered your primary residence.

Cons

- As with any financial product, fees can be convoluted and pricey.

- Salespeople often pair reverse mortgages with "investment opportunities" in an effort to generate commissions. As a rule of thumb, don't borrow against your home to invest in anything.

- Because a reverse mortgage is a debt, it can become immediately payable at default. In other words, if you don't follow the terms of the loan, such as paying your property taxes, you will be required to pay all of the money back or leave your home.

Good Debt/Bad Debt rating: 1

Analysis: I've come to think of reverse mortgages as defibrillation paddles. You know, "the restart your heart if your heart stops" paddles. A defibrillator can be the greatest thing in the world if your heart has stopped, but it can stop your heart if you don't actually need a jolt. Reverse mortgages are a fantastic last-ditch effort at solvency and stability, but if you aren't in desperate need of solvency and stability, then a reverse mortgage can create a desperate need for solvency and stability.

Proper planning can circumvent the need to suck equity back out of your home. But if you desperately need income and you own your home outright, then proceed cautiously through the world of reverse mortgages.

PERSONAL LOANS (FROM A FINANCIAL INSTITUTION)

A personal loan is an unsecured loan (meaning that you don't have to put up any collateral) granted for personal use. You might secure a personal loan to help pay for everything from medical expenses to replacing your home's air conditioner to covering college costs.

The loan amount is determined by your credit history and your income—essentially, your ability to pay back your lender. Because no collateral is involved, your interest rates will be much higher.

Good Debt/Bad Debt rating: 2

Analysis: It's possible you will need to take a personal loan from a bank, but you should try to avoid it. A personal loan is similar to a secured or an unsecured equity line, except a personal loan isn't open-ended and can have a shorter amortization schedule.

PERSONAL LOANS (FROM A FAMILY MEMBER OR FRIEND)

Do you love your family and friends? (The correct answer is yes.) Then why make your financial problems their financial problems? Personal loans from family and friends, whether formal or informal, are a bad idea. If a lending institution isn't willing to loan you money because of your credit-(un)worthiness, why subject your loved ones to your objectively high level of lending risk?

Your family and friends may offer to help you out financially, but unless it's life or death, say no. Relationships should not be splintered for avoidable financial reasons.

Good Debt/Bad Debt rating: 1

Analysis: Avoid both sides of the personal loans from friends or family equation. You will almost always come away disappointed.

TAX DEBT

Tax debt happens when you fail to pay earned income taxes to the state or federal government. In addition to the debt total, depending on the severity of the situation, you could incur fines and penalties (including jail time) for delayed payments.

If tax debt goes unpaid for long enough, the IRS has the right to garnish your wages until the debt is paid off. You might also have the ability to set up a payment plan with the IRS to pay off your debt in installments.

The moral of the story? Make sure you know how to calculate your personal and business taxes—or hire someone who can. That investment will more than offset the costs incurred from tax debt. You want stress? Owe the IRS back taxes. You want to avoid financial stress? Start by keeping current with your taxes. You don't want to go down the tax-debt road. It's a dead end.

Good Debt/Bad Debt rating: 1

Analysis: Did you read the part of this section that said jail time? Jail time is an automatic 1 on the Good Debt/Bad Debt rating scale.

COLLECTION DEBT

If you are unable to pay a bill, the lender can send it directly to a debt-collection agency. As a result, you'll begin to receive phone calls and letters from collectors in the weeks following your first missed payment. If you owe a substantial amount of money, debt collectors can take extreme measures—such as filing judgments—to ensure that you repay the debt.

Being unable to pay a bill is stressful in the first place; being sent to collections adds another level of financial stress that can affect your entire life.

Good Debt/Bad Debt rating: 1

Analysis: A strange yet common reaction to having debt go to collections is to ignore the collection calls. Don't ignore the collection calls. Unfortunately, when a debt goes to collections, you will lose leverage. The collection agents are generally compensated based on the amount of money they can collect from you. To move on with your financial life, you must right things with the collection companies that hold your debts. Don't let it get this far—but if it does, deal with it quickly.

JUDGMENTS

Judgments are legal obligations to pay a debt or damages that have been issued in a court of law. If a creditor takes you to court and is awarded a judgment, it gives the creditor the right to use additional methods to collect the debt they are owed, including wage garnishment, liens, and levies.

Wage garnishment involves an automatic deduction from your paycheck—up to 25 percent—each pay period. This money is sent directly to your judgment creditor until the debt is paid off.

The judgment process is quite nasty. Creditors often provide delinquent borrowers with a summons to appear in court. The hope for the creditors is that the borrower doesn't show up to court. When a borrower misses his or her time in front of a judge, the creditor is given a default judgment. This is when wages can be garnished. Creditors have been known to consistently seek continuances when borrowers actually show up for court, in order to increase the chances that a borrower won't show up for the next hearing. The second a borrower doesn't show up in court, a default judgment is made. A creditor's goal is to get a default judgment. Your goal is to not get anywhere close to being in this situation. And if you are in this situation, show up for court. Don't let a default judgment occur.

When a lien is placed on your home or your property, you will have to pay the debt with the money you earn from selling or refinancing the assets that have liens.

If the judgment creditor is awarded a levy, they can take funds directly from your checking or savings account—or even levy your personal property and sell it in an auction—to pay off the debt.

Good Debt/Bad Debt rating: 2

Analysis: Look, judgments aren't great. And I understand that having your wages garnished is both frustrating and embarrassing, but at least you'll get out of debt. Don't get me wrong; you should avoid letting your debts get so out of control that a judge is involved, but there is a silver lining to having your debts go to judgment: You will finally deal with the obligation you've been fighting or ignoring. You can't make progress when you're in denial. A judgment flips the denial switch to reality.

A CLOSER LOOK AT DEBT AND PAYING IT DOWN

Every bad habit comes equipped with a healthy dose of denial. Debt is no different. Over the years, I've compiled a mental archive of the different ways people try to rationalize their debt or blame it on someone else. Here are some of the most common:

▶ My finances were in good shape until I got those unexpected medical bills in the mail.

▶ I had to take out student loans because I didn't have a job.

▶ The TV was on sale. I would have been silly not to buy it at that price.

▶ My car was out of warranty, and I hate driving a car that isn't under warranty.

▶ I was throwing money away by renting, so it only made sense to buy a house.

▶ I wanted to build credit, so I opened a store credit card. And then it got a bit out of control.

The list goes on. But no matter how good your excuse is, there's no gray area when it comes to debt—you're either in it or you're not. And if you're in it, it can only be tackled through discipline, patience, and proper planning. As you begin to think about your debt, remember one thing: A debt is a debt is a debt. Don't ignore the "12 months same as cash" debt you accrued when you bought your new couch on the promise of no interest for a year. Don't ignore your student loans, even if they're in deferment. (While deferment does allow you to delay your payments, doing so simply puts off the inevitable.) If you owe money to any company, person, or other entity, it counts toward your debt total. Compartmentalizing your debt into arbitrary categories merely detracts from your progress.

Although I'm dedicating only one chapter to the creation of your debt pay-down plan, it could take months or even years to get completely out of debt, depending on the amount of debt you have. Don't be discouraged by the impending hard work, though; this plan will get you on a regular payment schedule, make your financial stress progressively easier to manage, and prepare you for your retirement income.

YOUR RELATIONSHIP WITH DEBT

Let's not be obtuse and suggest that all debt is bad. Debt exists in a person's life for several reasons. It may exist due to a lack of preparedness. It may exist due to poor behavior and decision-making. And it may exist as a reasonable strategy. But no matter the reason, debt consistently does one not-so-good thing: It obligates you to your past. In fact, every time you make the decision to go into debt, your current self is creating a relationship with your future self. It's hard enough to fund both your current lifestyle and your future life. If you throw in a relationship with your past financial decisions, then watch out.

DEBT PAY-DOWN PROCESS

Despite the challenges debt can present to a retirement plan, debt reduction just prior to retirement can create a very strange, yet positive, effect. When you commit to liquidating vast amounts of consumer debt, you almost always reduce your spending down to the essentials. Once you're committed to this methodology, the longer your spending is based on necessity, the better chance you have to shape your retirement spending habits. For example, let's say your current net monthly household income is $4,500. Of this income, let's say you have $1,600/month in debt payment obligations. What happens when those debt obligations go away? In a way, it means you need $19,200 ($1,600/month for 12 months) less income every year. Can you imagine if you matched this dip in income need with your retirement date? It would be magical. Okay, maybe not magical, but really smart.

You have this opportunity if you create this opportunity. For years, you may have been worrying about how your consumer debt would affect your ability to retire. However, your debt can actually help you adjust to your retirement income stream, and it can actually put you in a better position than those not dealing with consumer debt. The final years leading up to retirement are crucial for so many reasons, but none more so than learning to live on less discretionary income. A structured debt pay-down is the perfect way to accomplish this goal, but first we need to look at the type of attitude that creates debt.

People use three primary strategies to pay off debt. One of these strategies is effective; the other two strategies are commonly used yet often fall short. You must understand all three strategies, which we'll discuss in a moment, to understand why one strategy is the best.

Paying down debt is challenging for several reasons, but the two hardest parts are your battle against human nature and your simultaneous attack on your financial past, present, and future.

Before you get started with your debt pay-down, you need to understand a very important piece of the debt-reduction puzzle: You must stop using debt as a tool. It's impossible to get out of debt if you keep trickling back into debt each month by using your credit card. Stop using your bank credit card, store credit card, and/or line of credit. You won't be able to stay afloat if there's a hole in your boat.

Your commitment not to use debt as a tool will require sacrifice. Your credit card may have allowed you to buy some time in the past, but the time you bought came at a serious price. Now it's time to pay the piper.

Once you've committed to not using your credit cards, you are ready to get out of debt. The three most popular methods of paying off debt are the *math* method, the *momentum* method, and the *shotgun* method. Do you know which one is best?

THE MATH METHOD

Because debt deals with numbers, you'd think math would and should be involved in paying off debt. Well, it is, but at some point it makes sense to ignore the math and focus on your behavior instead. We'll talk more about that in a bit.

To be fair, the math method is technically the best way to pay off debt. But I find it to much less effective than other methods. The reality is, if you were so good at operating in purely mathematical terms, would you have all that debt in the first place? Probably not.

When using the math method of paying off debt, you focus on attacking the debt that has the highest interest rate. Each debt that you have has its own interest rate. Some of your debts may have interest rates less than 10 percent, some in excess of 10 percent, and some interest rates even skyrocket past 30 percent. The higher the interest rate, the more money you will end up paying your creditors if you continue to stay in debt to them. This higher borrowing cost over time causes many people to attack their debts with the highest interest rates first. And technically, they are doing the right thing. The faster they pay down the high-interest debts, the less interest they'll pay on those debts. It's textbook perfect. But human nature is a fickle beast.

Paying off your past financial decisions can prove so difficult and time consuming that you may abandon a successful strategy if you don't feel you're getting the results you desire in a timely manner. Behavior change needs to be reinforced. If you've shifted your financial habits to throw more money toward your debts, you want to see tangible, powerful results, right? Consider the following scenario.

You have two $2,000 debts. One is a car loan at 2.9 percent interest, and the other debt is a credit card at 29.99 percent interest. Which debt would you focus on paying off first? When I say "focus on," I mean paying more than the minimum required payment.

For this example, let's assume you have an additional $200 per month you could put toward one of your debts. If you used the highest interest rate method, you would attack the credit card, because its rate is 27.09 percent more than the car loan interest rate. But what do you think the minimum payment is for the credit card? Maybe $70 or so? Now, what do you think the payment on the car loan is? For the sake of the example, let's say $300. If you were to pay off the car loan first, you would free up $300 per month of cash flow. If you were to pay off the high-interest credit card first, you'd free up $70 per month of cash flow.

By ignoring the interest rates, you would be able to access $300 faster than you could access $70. Additionally, if you had been paying the $200 extra toward your car loan, then you would have been making $500 payments. You would already be used to living without the $500 with regard to discretionary spending, so you could simply start paying $570 per month toward your credit card balance once your car loan was paid off.

And just like that, you've dipped your toe into the waters of the momentum method....

THE MOMENTUM METHOD

The momentum method of paying off debt has been around for years, and people call it many different things. I call it the momentum method. It takes advantage of human behavior and engagement. Many people give up on their debt-repayment strategy because they don't see the fruits of their labor. The momentum method ensures that you will see your debts start to shrink in a dramatic and impactful way.

In a nutshell, the momentum method requires you to make minimum payments on all your debts, except your smallest-balance debt. You should then aggressively attack the smallest-balance debt, paying as much toward it as possible. Once it's eliminated, take its minimum payment and use it to focus on the next smallest debt, along with all the other income you've dedicated to debt repayment. Continue attacking the smallest-balance debt until all your debts are eliminated.

I prefer the momentum method and fully endorse it. I'll fully explain how it works after you understand the shotgun method.

THE SHOTGUN METHOD

Shotguns are effective because when you pull the trigger once, your target area is riddled with shot. The idea is that by peppering the target area, you are more likely to hit the intended specific target. A rifle, on the other hand, gives you one shot to hit the intended target. Yet from a distance, a rifle is a much more powerful weapon. Don't spray your debt from a distance with lots of little pellets.

The shotgun method of debt is when you attack many debts at once. Specifically, you pay more than the minimum payment on several different debts. I know you've always heard that you *should* pay more than your minimum payments on all your different debts, but you shouldn't. You will get out of debt much faster if you focus all of your extra payments toward your lowest-balance debt.

People who use the shotgun method often describe a sensation of running in place. A few years ago I met a nurse who was paying extra on all her different debts. She had nine credit cards, a car loan, and three medical bills. She was paying $1,500 per month toward her debts, yet she hadn't made much progress in more than two years. Upon discovering that she was using the shotgun method, we changed her strategy to the momentum method and ran some quick projections. In just two short months using the momentum method, she paid off five debts and freed up $450 of cash flow per month.

GETTING OUT OF DEBT

Eliminating a debt means eliminating a minimum payment. The faster you eliminate a debt, the faster you get to recapture its minimum payment. Because of this, your goal is to pay off debts as quickly as possible. The fastest way to do this is to attack the smallest-balance debt first. Here's how it works.

STEP 1: MAP OUT YOUR DEBT

Before you decide how you're going to pay off your debt, you need to figure out what debt you actually have. If you are in a bit of denial over your debts, you may have never compiled a comprehensive list. To do this, list all of your debts, from the smallest balance to the largest balance, in Table 2.1. Allow yourself as much time as necessary to complete this table—and make sure not to leave out any details. Remember to list every type of debt. This includes credit cards, mortgages, car loans, student loans, personal loans, and even debts that have made their way to collections.

STEP 2: BUILD MOMENTUM WITH SMALL DEBT VICTORIES

Don't make equal payments on each debt; it's inefficient. Employing this strategy may have been your problem for years. It's not unusual for people to pay extra on all their debts. As you know, your debts have a required minimum payment. Many people do what they believe to be a good idea and pay more than the minimum payment on all their debts. Frustration eventually sets in because they don't appear to be making any progress toward their goal of being debt free.

Table 2.1: Map Out Your Debt			
Whom Do You Owe?	**Amount Owed**	**Minimum Payment**	**New Monthly Payment**

Table 2.1: Map Out Your Debt

Whom Do You Owe?	Amount Owed	Minimum Payment	New Monthly Payment

Instead, you should focus on paying off your smallest debt and getting the balance down to zero. This will free up the money you were putting toward the monthly minimum payment so you can put it toward the next debt—not to mention it also helps you create a sense of financial momentum. You may start out by paying only $100 per month extra above the minimum payment. But by the end of the debt pay-down process, you might actually be putting upwards of $1,000 per month toward the next lowest debt balance. This scenario is possible because you have eliminated debts and are able to use former minimum payments to help you pay off the next debt.

If you're wondering why we're focusing on the lowest balance instead of the highest interest rate, it's because we're trying to create momentum and zero balances. So at this point, try not to concern yourself with the interest rates (even though I know that goes against conventional wisdom).

Creating small victories and zero balances up front is the financial equivalent of losing that first five pounds on a diet. You just need some confirmation that what you're doing really works. As you pay off these balances, you'll begin to accumulate the money you were once putting toward minimum payments each month, allowing you to apply those savings to the next lowest balance on your list.

STEP 3: COMMIT TO A DEBT-PAYMENT SCHEDULE

This process is as simple as it gets, assuming you commit to making it part of your routine. The key is to keep chipping away at the debt. Sure, it will take time, but it will also work. Every time you free up money in your budget, apply it to your next lowest balance.

As a personal finance expert, I'm always tempted to create complicated processes for debt liquidation. But the reality is you need a very simple plan that's easy to stick to. Debt liquidation is way too important to complicate it with confusing financial algorithms and impossible goals.

YOUR PERSPECTIVE NEEDS TO SHIFT

There's no doubt your debt is a hindrance. But if you shift your perspective, then this hindrance immediately becomes a legitimate opportunity. This isn't some sort of strange exercise in semantics. If you pay down your debt between now and your retirement date, it may actually put you in a better position over those that are spending a vast majority of their pre-retirement income on consumer habits that have been formed for a decade or more. Whereas those people are forcing themselves to quit a learned habit, you are employing brilliant, healthy habits as you head into your retirement.

People often take on debt payments based on consumer confidence. When your world is great, when the economy is singing and the market is climbing, most people feel confident. Confidence is a great thing, but what generally happens next isn't. Consumer confidence is used as an economic measure for economists because purchasing usually follows it. When confident, a person tends to spend money, not save money. When people lack confidence, they save money. I know; it's a terribly backward way of thinking. Don't waste confidence on creating more obligations. Harness confidence to improve your life, not your lifestyle.

A NOTE ON CREDIT SCORES

I have a secret. I'm going to share it with you, but you must be willing to ignore everything you've heard about the importance of credit scores. The older you get, the less your credit score actually matters.

What does a credit score measure? It measures how good you are at borrowing money. I don't want to be good at borrowing money, because I don't want to borrow money. Sure, you'll need to borrow money to buy your home, but aside from that it's quite possible to live your life without really borrowing money. The challenge is that to borrow money for something like a house, you need to demonstrate your ability to successfully borrow smaller amounts of money. Seems simple, right? Nope. At one point in time, it *was* that simple. Today? Well, it's no longer simple. Credit scores today do more to induce borrowing than they do to discourage borrowing.

If I had to oversimplify a healthy timeline of a person's relationship with debt, it would go like this: Establish credit, buy a house, and then be done with credit. Every day, people all around the world make this choice. Whether you choose to do so is up to you. But it wouldn't be fair for me to leave our discussion on credit at that. You need to understand how the system works, regardless of whether you choose to be part of it.

Your borrowing career should be over. And in turn, your credit career should be over. Frankly, there's not a tremendous amount of utility or practicality in establishing and catering to your credit score when you're in your fifties.

YOUR CHILDREN'S CREDIT

While your relationship with credit and debt may be coming to a sweet end, if you have children who are on the cusp of adulthood, then they are likely to be in the courtship phase of their relationship with credit. It is important for you to support them in their efforts to establish credit; however, it's very important that you don't *support* them in their efforts to establish credit.

As you may or may not know, some lending institutions may ask for a cosigner when the primary borrower doesn't appear to be a good credit risk. And if your young-adult children have no credit, then they are viewed as a high credit risk. Lending institutions generally aren't willing to take on the risks associated with someone with no credit history, and that's why they want someone else to take the risk: you. The lender wants you to cosign so you assume the risk of the borrower.

When you become a cosigner, you are essentially promising to pay back the loan if the primary borrower can't handle the loan payments. At first glance, it doesn't necessarily sound like a terrible idea, but it is. With very few exceptions, I find cosigning to be an irresponsible step to take, for both you and your adult child.

You shouldn't take on a risk that a lending institution isn't willing to take on. And you shouldn't help your kids circumvent a very important step in the credit process. Your children need to learn how to handle credit and debt. They need to learn these concepts from the ground up. If you jump into the fray with them and remove an important step in the process, then how are you helping them? I frequently see an extension of this same problem when parents gift or loan down-payment money to their adult children to help them purchase their first home. Creating the illusion of financial stability isn't a step toward financial stability, it's a step toward danger.

I believe most people are put in a tough situation when asked to cosign, and they generally acquiesce due to guilt. Don't get me wrong; there's a ton of pressure and emotion revolving around cosigning. "Don't you trust me?" the borrower might ask. But cosigning isn't about trust, it's about risk. Risk and trust have very little to do with each other. Do you know who specializes in risk assessment? Lending institutions. Do you know who *doesn't* specialize in risk assessment? Biased family members. As much scrutiny and criticism as banks receive, they still serve an important purpose with regard to loan underwriting. If a bank says no, then why should you say yes? When you cosign, you are essentially underwriting a sub-prime loan. This is tricky territory. People love to get mad at banks for loaning money to people they shouldn't. Why would you loan money to someone you shouldn't?

This isn't a credit score discussion, either. Earlier this year, a young guy came to me with no credit. In the eyes of the credit agencies, he hadn't done enough to register a blip on their screens. I started poking around this guy's finances and quickly realized that he was doing a remarkable job making financial decisions. He had very few financial obligations, and he had accumulated $50,000 in savings. He wanted to buy a home. I directed him to a lending institution that I knew would assess the risk involved with lending to someone with no credit. They assessed the risk and decided that his credit score, or lack thereof, was irrelevant. They loaned him money to buy a house.

As clichéd as this has become, isn't this an extension of the participation-trophy problem? There's no way that every kid deserves a trophy, and there's no way everyone has earned the right to borrow money. Not everyone has proven himself or herself to be a good risk. Family members shouldn't mess up this financial natural selection. Your kids aren't missing out when a bank tells them no. It's feedback. Your kids are being told they haven't done enough to display their credit worthiness. Credit rejection isn't a bad thing. When someone is denied a loan, it should be celebrated. Unfortunately, most people view a loan declination as some sort of insult. It's not. They should take no for an answer. Take that no, work on their skills, and then come back later to get a yes. How long will your child need to wait? Longer than he or she wants to. But that's okay.

It's not that different from letting your kid ride a carnival ride even if he or she isn't quite tall enough. Sure, you can probably talk your way past the carnie, but should you?

WHAT IF YOUR KIDS HAVE NO CREDIT AT ALL?

Credit cards are unnecessary once you have an established credit history. And in fact, I believe regular credit card use induces superfluous spending. Points, cash back, and other reward programs wouldn't exist if they didn't increase bank revenue via increased consumerism. This is exactly why I don't use a credit card and why I urge other established individuals to avoid using them. However, I do believe that a credit card is incredibly necessary to establish credit for those individuals who have no credit, especially your young-adult children.

Two groups of people want their credit score to go up: people with damaged credit and people with no credit. We've already discussed improving damaged credit, but now we'll discuss establishing credit when you, or your children, have none. When you have no credit, life can get incredibly difficult and frustrating. A person with no credit simply hasn't borrowed money that is reflected on his or her credit report. This leads to denials for new credit, increased rental costs, and the need for a cosigner. Which brings us to possibly the most frustrating question in personal finance: How in the world are people supposed to establish credit if they keep getting denied because they don't have any established credit?

The answer to this question is so shockingly simple that your head will spin. They need to get a credit card. I know; they've already tried that. But they did it wrong. Before we go much further, I need to draw a line in the sand. While I don't believe people with established credit should use a credit card, I *do* believe people with no credit should use a credit card to establish credit. I realize you might think I'm splitting hairs to make a point, but I assure you I'm not. Think of it this way: Your kids needed training wheels when they first learned to ride their bikes, yet they don't use them now. They *could* use them. There are still advantages to using them, but they don't. This is exactly what people with no established credit need to do with a credit card. They just need the right type of credit card.

Your kids need a secured credit card. A secured credit card is secured by a cash deposit. Specifically, they send the credit card company a check or money order for $200 to $1,000 to secure the credit line. The credit card company doesn't have to trust that they will pay their credit card bill, because they already have the person's money. Think of it like a refillable gift card that reports to the credit agencies. When your kids make a purchase, they create a debt on the card. To establish a credit history, they will make a payment on that debt to bring their security deposit back to its original amount. For instance, if they start with a $200 security deposit, spend $50 on shoes, then at the end of the month send $50 to the credit card company to take their balance back to the $200 deposited, the bank will report this credit activity to the credit agencies. This establishes credit in a safe way. And did I mention that your kids will get their deposit back when they're finished? No, of course I didn't mention that until now.

The point of this exercise isn't to buy things that they can't afford. The point is to buy things they *can* afford and then demonstrate their ability to pay back their debts on schedule.

There are some other considerations. Your kids shouldn't leave a balance on the card greater than 50 percent of the entire credit line. For example, if they have $200 deposited, they shouldn't build up debts over $99. If they do, they will have a high credit utilization ratio, and this can affect their credit score negatively. Additionally, they will need/want to continue putting small purchases on this card for about 12 months to establish credit. They can always deposit more cash into the security deposit to increase their credit line, but they shouldn't get too carried away. The point of this exercise is to establish their credit for a few very important reasons, which we'll discuss in a moment. Oh, and they better not miss a payment. They will go from having no credit to having damaged credit, and that's a transition they don't want to make.

When your kids have no credit, their auto insurance, renters insurance, and homeowners insurance costs can be higher than they would be otherwise. If they have no credit, they may have trouble renting a home or an apartment. And if they have no credit, it will be very difficult for them to get a mortgage, no matter how great the rest of their financial life is. Some financial institutions do something called *manual underwriting*. This is a loan-evaluation process in which a person's non-credit factors are weighed differently from a conventional underwriting process. And while I've seen individuals utilize this process in the past, it's no sure thing.

Establishing credit will let your children do all sorts of other things. However, many of these things aren't so great. Established credit will allow them to get store credit cards, car loans, and unsecured credit cards. I find all three of these uses of credit to be unnecessary. They used training wheels to learn to ride a bike; make sure to tell them to take off the training wheels once they learn to ride.

WHAT NOW?

The fewer obligations you have, the less pressure you will put on your income. Your goal is to permanently eliminate as many (debt) obligations as possible. There is a hidden benefit to paying off your debts systematically using the momentum method. You will learn to live without the money you use to pay on your debts' principal and interest each month. The first month you are debt free will determine what's next for you and your financial life.

If, upon becoming debt free, you reabsorb the money you've put toward debt reduction, you'll waste a giant opportunity. The most dangerous month in your financial recovery is always the month after you become debt free, because if you form new habits with your new discretionary income, then you are creating new forms of obligations. Instead, focus on making the best use of your freed-up capital. Strengthen your emergency fund. Increase your contributions to your retirement plan. Do anything to move yourself forward. Don't create new obligations.

CHAPTER 3

THE PRESENT: SPENDING

Truth be told, you think you want margin. You want to make more money in any given month than you spend in any given month. Not to get weird here, but that's technically the only financial advice anyone ever needs to hear. But it's stupefying to think how hard it is to turn this simple financial concept into the average person's reality. I'm sure there are many reasons for this, but among them has to be our penchant for picking our expenses before our incomes are determined. And don't forget about how good we've gotten at spending our gross income, in spite of the limited availability of our net income.

Margin is sneaky, though. It can be right in front of your face, and you'll have no idea what you're really looking at. Take, for instance, how quickly your newly paid-off car's former payment gets absorbed into your life. Think about the two months per year in which you receive three paychecks instead of two, if you happen to be on a 26-pay schedule. Think about the time you checked your checking account balance minutes before you went out shopping. Think about your tax refund check, end-of-the-year bonus, or pay rate increase. Did you view any of these opportunities as margin creation, or did you view these opportunities as something else? Basically, we talk ourselves out of creating margin.

I fought for margin for years. The harder I fought, the more mysteriously distant margin became. And then it hit me: I don't want margin, I want to save money. There's a huge difference. If you're seeking margin, you're seeking a gap in your income and expenses that can be used for whatever you want. But if you had trouble finding and creating margin in the first place, then chances are you didn't always make the best decisions with the money that was available to do whatever you wanted with. You've always hoped that you'll save money if given the chance, but when given the chance you haven't actually saved money. You've convinced yourself that the money had a better purpose than being saved. Good, bad, or otherwise, this was the decision you made. I know this because this was the decision that I kept making over and over and over again.

You don't want margin; you want to save money. Stop seeking margin and start saving money. Start making fewer resources available for discretionary spending. You can do this by depositing money into a savings account on a bimonthly basis. If you're like me, then you just asked whether bimonthly means twice per month or every other month. I don't know either. But do it twice per month. And by the way, it's really hard to permanently save money when your checking and savings accounts are linked. The link is a conduit for money to flow back and forth. The forth isn't so bad, but the back will kill you. If you want saved money to stay saved, close the door behind it.

CASH FLOW

You'll never know for sure what's going on with your money unless you track it. Controlling your cash flow is the single most financially responsible thing you can do. When people say you need to learn to walk before you learn to run, they are describing this very concept. Understanding cash flow is a fundamental financial baby step, yet it's the one thing people gleefully ignore.

Often, the more money you make, the more you ignore cash-flow management. When you feel broke, you usually do something about it (in other words, you monitor your cash flow). But when you feel financially prosperous, you may not feel as concerned about where your money goes. This principle is what typically prevents people who have increased their income from increasing their wealth. And while consistently increasing your spending to match your income throughout your career is troubling, it can turn into a nightmare during retirement. Because for all intents and purposes, you gain access to your entire life savings the moment you turn 59-1/2. What happens when you retire and you gain access to all the money you are likely to ever have—and you have 168 hours per week to spend it? If you haven't mastered healthy money management habits, what happens is shortage after shortage after shortage.

Cash flow describes the flow of money into your household (income) and the flow of money out of your household (expenses). A positive net cash flow means you have more money coming in than going out, and a negative net cash flow means you have more money going out than coming in. These net cash flows are also known, respectively, as a *surplus* and a *shortage*. In addition, it's important that you don't keep too much money at your disposal. Whether intentionally or accidentally, many people experience manufactured financial tranquility as a result of keeping too much money in their checking accounts. While this may sound like a good problem to have, it is dangerous. A checking account has a very low yield, meaning your money gains only a minimal amount of interest when instead it could be working for you. But more importantly and less obviously, keeping too much money at your disposal can ruin an otherwise perfectly good financial situation.

Let me explain by using my favorite bathroom resource—toilet paper—as an example. As unpleasant as it is to think about, we've all been faced with the alarming prospect of being stranded without the appropriate amount of toilet paper. It may sound humorous now, but it's extremely unfunny in the moment. The point is, faced with the cardboard, you will survive in any way possible, and you'll learn two lessons because of it:

▶ Check supply levels before you use the bathroom!

▶ Be resourceful.

It's easy to be wasteful when you have a full roll and you forget what you went through when faced with an empty roll.

The same thing can happen when you have a relatively large roll, er, balance in your checking account. This feeling of financial abundance can occur with as little as $100 or $200 "extra" in your checking account. The amount of money that causes this strangely damaging phenomenon is different for everyone. It all depends on at what amount you start to be relatively complacent.

Think about your checking account. At what point do you stop checking the balance in your head before making a purchase? When you have a cushion of $100? $200? $500? When you become comfortable with your cushion, your economic stress eases, and you start making spending decisions that aren't always prudent or even practical. This is what I like to call *abundance spending*, and it can manifest itself in several ways.

A feeling of financial comfort can lead you to buy items normally out of your price range for one very simple reason: You know you presently have the money to cover them. The larger the cushion you give yourself, the larger the financial mistakes you can make. For example, think about all of the celebrities and once-well-off public figures who have gone bankrupt. When you hear these stories, you wonder how someone who once had so much could now have next to nothing. I'm not a betting man (but you probably already knew that), but I'd guess that in 99 percent of these cases, abundance mentality played a very large role.

But back to the concept of cash flow. You can increase yours in two ways:

- ▶ Spend less money by controlling your expenses.
- ▶ Make more money.

Despite popular belief, more money is not always the solution to your financial problems. When you give an undisciplined person more money, he or she is likely to end up in financial trouble again. The solution to what ails you is not more money—it's spending less. So if you want to improve your monthly cash flow, start by cutting your expenses. Otherwise, you are filling your money bucket with more money...despite the fact that there is a hole in your bucket.

HOW USING A CREDIT CARD COMPLICATES SPENDING

I frequently encounter people who want to argue the "charge everything and pay it off at the end of the month" method with me. This method has a person put every single monthly expense, even utility bills, on his or her credit card and then make one big payment to pay off the credit card balance each month. People do this for several reasons, including earning credit card points, increasing their credit scores, and creating convenience. And while using this particular method of spending accomplishes all three of those things, it's still a bad idea.

The credit card usage proponents will tell you about all the rewards they earn. They'll tell you how they've paid for Christmas gifts with the rewards points they receive, and they'll go into great detail about how committed they are to paying off their entire balance at the end of each month. But what they don't realize is that their logic has failed them. The discipline that's required to pay off a card at the end of every month opens them up to a lack of financial accountability throughout the month. Their commitment to pay off their debt at the end of each month—no matter how much it is—is exactly what gets them in trouble.

Here's why:

► **People rarely check their credit card balance mid-month.** On the other hand, people who do most of their spending with their checking account generally check their account balances at least twice (and generally more like 10 times) per month. While monitoring your checking account balance isn't exactly the perfect way to watch your spending, it's much better than never checking your balance—especially if you're trying to live lean and cut spending.

People who charge everything and then worry about it later (at the end of the month) don't really care how much they've spent mid-month because they aren't in danger of having insufficient funds. The "charge everything and pay it off at the end of the month" people never approach their credit card limit during the course of the month. This means that spending habits gone awry aren't addressed until the behavior has passed.

This isn't good. You should study your spending habits. How? By monitoring your spending. Have you ever had one of those weeks where stress, a sense of abundance, or the commerce fairy has caused you to spend money like it was going out of style? Join the club. Everyone has. But when you charge everything and pay it off at the end of the month, you tend to ignore this problem until the billing cycle is over. No one ever goes on a three-day spending bender and then checks their credit card balance mid–billing cycle.

▶ **When you're using a credit card, spending is much less consistent.** Scarcity is one of the best financial tools on the planet. I personally use it all the time to accomplish very important personal financial goals. However, when you exclusively use your credit card to buy things, you kick scarcity out of the equation. What's your credit card limit? Five thousand dollars? Ten thousand? Fifteen thousand? That's about typical for someone who uses the "charge everything and pay it off at the end of the month" method.

For the sake of conversation, let's say you put $4,000 per month on your credit card. Because you plan on paying off your credit card bill at the end of the month, you have at least $4,000 in your checking account, right? And what is even more likely is that you have much more than $4,000 in your checking account prior to paying your mortgage and credit card bill. How do I know this? Because about 40 percent of your spending is discretionary spending. You know, the type of spending that you put on your credit card.

My point? Between your swollen checking account and your $15,000 credit limit, you have "access" to $25,000 per month. This is a drain on anyone's self-control. You can afford *anything* you want. It is my experience both as an individual consumer and as someone who studies money that this access is a very, very bad thing.

Right now you might be thinking, "No way, Pete. I've never even considered that I have access to $25,000." Yes you have. Your brain has. Let's say you go to your sister's house for Thanksgiving dinner, and she has a bowl of M&Ms out for everyone to enjoy. In the first scenario, she has one four-ounce bag of M&Ms in a small dish for your entire family to pick at throughout the day. How do most people address this situation? They pick up just a few M&Ms with their fingertips. In the second scenario, your sister went to Costco. She has an entire three-gallon punchbowl filled with M&Ms. How do most people deal with this scenario? They jam their fist so far into the bowl that it looks like they're trying to rehab a shoulder injury. The large punchbowl filled with M&Ms will result in more consumption *every single time*. Yet your hunger never changed. *Nothing* changed except your snap judgment on the resources that were made available to you.

Scarcity will help you accomplish financial goals much more than abundance will. By the way, don't try to impress me with your giant credit limit. I'd be much more impressed if you didn't have a credit card at all.

▶ **You think you're beating the system.** Much like the guy who has a "system" for winning consistently at roulette, "charge everything and pay it off at the end of the month" people tend to think they are smarter than the house. The house *always* wins. Do you really think these multibillion-dollar companies with their marketing and consumer behavior research departments are giving you free stuff? Oh, come on. They are counting on you overspending—or better yet, they're waiting for your commitment to pay off your balance every month to fade. When it fades, then the interest clock starts. And don't think the credit card companies don't make money off of you if you pay off your balance. They have other revenue streams attached to your purchases, such as swipe fees.

Need more convincing? Okay, you asked for it.

Failed logic #1: I get 1 percent cash back on purchases. How is that bad?

Many credit card companies now offer you cash back on your purchases. This means that you'll receive somewhere between 1 and 3 percent of what you charge on the card in the form of a bill credit or a check from the credit card company. This is much less exciting than it seems. How much money do you spend each month on your credit card? Twenty-five hundred dollars? Thirty-five hundred? Let's say you put $2,500 per month on your credit card. What is 1 percent of $2,500? Twenty-five dollars. Wow, that's amazing. You received 25 whole American dollars for risking so much more.

What are the chances that you overspend by more than 1 percent each month on your credit card? I would say that chances are about 100 percent. As we discussed just a few moments ago, access to copious amounts of money is a bad thing when it comes to controlling spending. People who employ the "charge everything and pay it off at the end of the month" method tend to overspend by at least 10 percent per month. This means that your 1 percent or even 3 percent cash back is pointless. You are actually behind by between 7 and 9 percent per month. You'd be better off not using a credit card and mailing 5 percent of your money to the Easter Bunny.

Failed logic #2: I make enough money and spend enough money to make the rewards worth it.

Once again, high income doesn't necessarily mean you are a financial genius. It just means that you make a lot of money. So you have immediately said to yourself, "I spend much more than $2,500 on my credit card. I spend closer to $10,000 per month on my card." The percentages didn't change. Your cash back "reward" would be $100 per month, and your likely amount of financial waste would be $1,000 per month. You can't spend your way out of trouble. You cannot out-math math.

IF NOT A CREDIT CARD, THEN WHAT?

There once was a time when people balanced their checkbooks. It was called the 1980s. Back then, there were fewer ways to make a financial transaction. Your options were cash, check, and charge. You received your canceled checks in the mail, so you knew when your party was paid. The reality is we'd actually be in a better place if we still balanced our checkbooks, but most people don't. Technology has created convenience, and this convenience has created a new type of ignorance. If you happen to still balance your checkbook, keep doing it. Just know that the generations that have fallen in line behind you stopped balancing their checkbooks a long time ago.

Two convenient yet overused items emerged in the 1990s: the fanny pack and the debit card. While the fanny pack certainly is convenient, its insistence that you store things much in the way a marsupial would leaves me wanting more out of my containment solutions. And the debit card is the height of convenience. If you don't have cash, you can put a purchase on the plastic, and it's automatically withdrawn from your checking account. You don't need to carry around a checkbook, and more than one accountholder can use the cards at the same time, in multiple locations.

You would think the only prerequisite would be having money in your checking account to cover the purchases. Alas, this isn't the case, because that would make too much sense. Why would a bank offer you convenience if it doesn't improve its bottom line? It generally wouldn't. Banks make billions of dollars every year on debit card fees and overdraft fees. Therefore, they will often let you spend money you don't have, charge you overdraft fees, and then create a massive debt that must be satisfied the next time you deposit money into your account.

Fast-food restaurants accept debit cards, carwashes accept debit cards, and even the telephone company accepts debit cards. Thanks to the debit card, the critical thinking that used to guide our financial decision-making has decreased, while our number of financial transactions has increased.

Misusing your debit cards (and make no mistake about it, this is misuse) is the same as misusing cash. But when you run out of cash, you stop spending it. At times, a debit card can be just as bad as a credit card, but instead of paying interest you pay pricey overdraft fees. What's the solution? Make a commitment to discipline. If you are going to enjoy the convenience of a debit card, you should be willing to track every purchase against your budget on a monthly basis. It is nearly impossible to keep a mental note on more than 90 transactions during the course of a month.

On top of the problems you create for yourself via frequent debit card use, your bank can create problems for you as well. As of 2012, many financial institutions have started increasing the fees associated with debit card accounts. In many instances, these institutions are charging between 75 cents and $1.50 every time you enter your debit card PIN (personal identification number). This means every time you withdraw money out of the ATM or every time you enter your PIN to purchase something at a store, you are a creating a fee. You can easily rack up $50 per month in these silly fees if you have a debit card usage-frequency issue.

I still believe utilizing a debit card is the best choice, despite the problems it can cause. If you can curtail the mistakes and not get addicted to swiping it, then your debit card can provide the perfect combination of convenience and practicality.

SHOULD YOU SELECT DEBIT OR CREDIT WHEN SWIPING YOUR DEBIT CARD?

I'm sure you've noticed that you can often choose whether to run your debit card as a credit card or a debit card. Have you wondered what the difference is? Here's what happens when you run your debit card as a debit, and here's what happens when you run your debit card as a credit card. In the spirit of full disclosure, I almost always select debit because I think it's fairer to the merchant, and I don't like having a delay in payment processing.

Running as debit:

▶ Doing so requires you type in your four-digit PIN.

▶ It's the only way to get cash back with no ATM fees.

▶ From a merchant's perspective, this is the closest you can get to paying with cash.

▶ Fees are minimal to a merchant, and it benefits them for you to use this option. These transactions are considered "online," and your purchase will automatically be deducted from your account.

▶ Because these transactions are run through STAR or NYCE, they aren't offered the extra protection of a credit card, though your bank protects all funds in your checking account.

▶ In a few rare cases, banks limit debit transactions per month or you are charged fees for using debit. Why? You'll see in the next section.

Running debit as credit:

▶ Considered an "offline" purchase, transactions run this way most likely won't come out of your account immediately, but will be charged in a batch in the evening when the store closes, though this varies by merchant.

▶ Banks especially benefit from debit cards used as credit because the merchant is charged higher fees that go directly to the bank. This is actually a huge source of revenue for the bank.

▶ Because banks benefit from you running your debit card as credit, they will often offer rewards or incentives for choosing this method.

▶ You'll notice your debit card has the Visa or MasterCard logo on it. This means when your debit card is run as credit, it is backed by this company. For example, if your debit card is backed by Visa, you are eligible for their zero-liability policy.

▶ To cover the high fees charged to the merchant, those fees are often passed back to you, the consumer, in the form of higher prices and/or minimum purchase limits for paying with plastic.

HOW DO YOU ACTUALLY REDUCE SPENDING?

Some people may define financial progress as "being able to afford more." I define it differently, as "needing less money to live."

The fewer financial obligations you have, the more freedom you have. Yet, in part due to the influence of marketing and the media, Americans tend to add obligations as they increase their income and their wealth. If you measure your success by what you have, you're in deep trouble. This isn't cause for panic, though, because you can adjust this attitude. Your spending habits, no matter how deep-seated they are, can change. They *must* change, especially if they are the roadblocks standing in the way of your financial progress.

Not only do you need to change your current "fixed" spending habits, you also must reduce the number of financial obligations you have and those you continue to accept. By making some subtle changes that will have a major impact on your bottom line, you can easily reclaim thousands of dollars per year from your budget.

The following four spending categories can immediately reflect your growing financial awareness (or lack thereof):

► Groceries

► Dining out

► Utilities

► The new necessities

GROCERIES

The grocery store is a microcosm of your world when it comes to spending decisions. In this microcosm, you can isolate certain behaviors and decision-making processes, analyze them, and then use the resulting data to alter your financial behaviors in all spending situations.

Do you make impulsive purchases or stick to your grocery list? Are you easily distracted by shiny and sparkly items? These are the type of questions you will consider when analyzing your grocery-store habits.

Good decisions at the grocery store can benefit you in two ways.

- ▶ They can directly and positively affect your finances in specific areas of your life.

  - ▶ By planning meals based on what's on sale and in season, you can reduce your impulse buying, over-spending, and food waste. Buying in season and local reduces food transportation costs, thus reducing your cost.

  - ▶ You can decrease your healthcare costs by making proper food choices.

  - ▶ If you can become immune to catchy but often meaningless grocery-store marketing tactics (such as flashy packaging and strategic shelf placement), you can apply the same discretion to other such tactics that appeal more to your senses than to your needs.

- ▶ They can help you develop the following good habits, which will carry over to all financial decisions:

  - ▶ Frugality

  - ▶ Willpower

  - ▶ Strategic planning and execution

  - ▶ Prioritizing

  - ▶ Budgeting and problem solving

If it seems like I'm putting a lot of pressure on your trip to the grocery store, that's because I am. Whereas you've no doubt come to consider these trips a means of picking up food for dinner, I'm focused on the part they play in a much grander financial plan.

Think about it. When you walk through a grocery store, one particular concept is abundantly clear: choice. You could buy anything you want, but should you? You could look for deals, but will your desire for instant gratification trump your need for a good bargain? You could buy brand names, but generic is cheaper and not very different (if at all) from brand-name items. You get to choose how much your compulsions will cost you and how much money you need for instant gratification.

DINING OUT

Not only is dining out convenient, it's fun. No shopping for hard-to-find ingredients, no lengthy preparation, and perhaps best of all, no cleanup.

Unfortunately, if you don't have a grasp on how dining out affects your financial life, you could be in for a great deal of trouble long after you pay the bill. I once witnessed a newly retired client spend 12 percent of his wealth in the first year of retirement because he insisted on dining out for three meals per day.

Sixty-six percent of American adults say they dine in a restaurant at least once a week. A statistic like this one no doubt results in large part from our hectic work schedules. If you're a member of the great American rat race like I am, sometimes you simply don't have the time or the energy to go grocery shopping and prepare adequate meals. On the other hand, if you're working incredibly long hours to sustain your indulgent dining habits, then you might be in the middle of a nasty cycle. (If you're just a workaholic, that's a completely different issue altogether.) If you are retired and not part of the rat race, then the excuse of not having time to make dinner goes out the window.

Yet to many, dining out is not only a source of sustenance, it's a primary source of entertainment. Both of these situations are common and fair. But no matter how you look at it, you should be fully aware of how dining out affects your personal bottom line.

The absolute best way to curb your spending on dining out is to track it on a weekly basis. This means giving yourself a weekly dining-out budget. Whether it's $75 or $20, it's much easier to keep track of the 21 meals in a week than it is to keep track of the 93 meals in a month.

UTILITIES

You can apply the same discipline you develop in other areas of your financial life to reducing your utility expenses. The average American has upwards of six or seven fixed expenses each month, including utility bills. But how much attention do you give your utility bills each month?

If you're like most Americans, probably not much. We tend to take the cost of "fixed" bills like these for granted. But are utility bills really fixed? Not really. Your habits, knowledge, and overall awareness can affect them, and you can reduce your utility costs with very little effort. So what do you say? Would you tweak a couple of your habits if it meant freeing up $300 per year? I thought you would.

Take the time to explore the various money-saving programs your different utility providers offer (but which they may not always go out of their way to advertise). For instance, can you bundle your different services? Can you switch to budget billing to avoid seasonal spikes on your bill?

Familiarize yourself with your utility providers' different payment options, either by calling the companies or by visiting their websites. Compare those options to the amount you pay monthly. Are you spending more than necessary to get the services you need? If so, make changes if doing so will ultimately save you money, and then watch the savings happen over the next few months.

You need to manage your utility bills in the same way you manage your assets. Because changing your financial life is all about changing your habits, adopt the following money-saving and energy-saving habits:

▶ **Consider installing a programmable thermostat.** This allows you to be energy efficient when you're away from your home during the day. If you don't have a programmable thermostat, settle on a temperature a few degrees lower (during winter) and higher (during summer) than you're used to. You'll be surprised by how much you can save.

▶ **Turn off your lights when you leave a room.** This is such an easy and obvious way to conserve energy and save money—yet few people do it. There's no need to keep lights on in unoccupied rooms, and there's really no reason to light your front lawn or backyard at night. If you're concerned about intruders or safety, consider switching to motion-detecting lights, which can lead to significant savings over time.

▶ **Conserve water.** Even if your water company doesn't offer an incentive to adopt water-conservation strategies, the potential savings should be incentive enough. Switching to low-flow shower heads and aerated faucets and adding "float boosters" to your toilet tank are great ways for homeowners to lower their water bills.

▶ **Unplug appliances and other devices that use energy when not in use.** This includes your television, toaster, cell-phone charger, and hair dryer. Also, turn off surge protectors and power strips when you're not using the electronics plugged into them. Keeping these items plugged in wastes energy and money.

▶ **Evaluate your need for a home phone.** Sometimes a cell phone can replace a traditional one entirely. Many people no longer need a landline but keep it because they don't want to get rid of a phone number they've had for years. But paying the phone company a fixed amount every month simply for the privilege of having a sentimental phone number and a service you can live without is a lot more painful than the steps you can take to replace your home phone with your cell phone once and for all. If you already have a cell phone and are ready to make the switch, start by emailing your contacts your new number. Next, put your cell phone number on your landline voicemail or answering machine for a month prior to turning off your home phone service. Finally, personally call those you want to have your new number (and skip those you don't!).

▶ **Check for air leaks around windows, doors, seal cracks, and drafty spaces.** Why spend time and money heating or air conditioning your home if the air is escaping? The principle of preventing waste alone should motivate you to investigate your home's efficiency. The principle of saving money is icing on the cake.

These steps may seem minor, but the small things truly do have the largest effects. In my experience, making these changes can save you as much as $300 per year, which you can put toward real financial priorities.

Gabe's story clearly illustrates how these tactics can save money. Gabe, a school counselor and summertime landscaper, always had budgeting problems. During the winter, his problem was particularly pronounced: Heating costs stretched his paycheck so thin that he was constantly hit with overdraft charges. Because one of his jobs was seasonal, his income was higher during the summer (and his heating bills were obviously lower as well). So his real issue wasn't budgeting, but timing—and awareness. He admitted he had never taken the time to consider how his utility bills could be affected by his habits and decisions—he had just come to accept high heating bills in winter as a fact of life.

The solution? He took five minutes to contact his natural gas provider and sign up for their budget-billing program. The program, which spreads heating costs over the entire year's bills, allowed him to pay a consistent amount each month. Instead of having his bill fluctuate between $50 and $400 each month, depending on the season, he paid a fixed fee of $150 per month. This fixed bill didn't eliminate any of Gabe's debt per se, but it did make it easier for him to budget year-round, which drastically improved his ability to focus on his financial goals and the other areas of his budget that needed attention.

THE NEW NECESSITIES

Without a real grasp of their traditional costs (such as utilities)—the majority of Americans have begun justifying the addition of new fixed expenses as well. I'm not going to make the case for getting rid of things you consider necessities—although you should certainly consider it if you're in debt—but they can add up and drain your checking account if each expense isn't monitored carefully. Perhaps the first question you should ask yourself is whether all of your necessities are, in fact, necessities.

Chances are, you have a greater number of "basic life necessities" than you did 10 or 20 years ago—and your list of basic "needs" is probably drastically larger than that of your parents. This is due to what I call the *Simplicity-Needs Paradox*, the contradiction presented when, in taking steps to simplify your life by decreasing the amount of energy you expend on routine tasks, you increase the number of basic needs necessary to maintain your new level of simplicity.

For example, email is far faster than snail mail, but to have access to email, you have to have a computer. Thus, to simplify you have to acquire. As you simplify your financial life, you'll have to account for the new necessities that have become basic needs. But with so many new necessities, how are you ever going to free up enough money to start saving? The basic fact of the matter is, you can't start saving until you stop spending.

IS IT EVER OKAY TO SPLURGE?

All of this financial restraint can build up some really strange feelings. You may be tempted to blow money.

Whereas being financially responsible can be addicting, sometimes you just want to spend money. It's important to acknowledge this desire and learn how to deal with it. Frankly, sometimes it's okay to splurge. You just need to set some ground rules to prevent the splurge from turning into a disaster.

▶ **Don't splurge to make yourself feel better about a bad financial situation.** Splurging in the midst of financial struggles is a bad idea. Once the high wears off from the splurge, reality will be all up in your face. A good way to splurge when you are broke is to splurge with another resource: time. Take the day to yourself. Go to a park and walk around. Go walk around the mall (but don't splurge). Just collect your thoughts and enjoy the silence. (It's quite obvious at this point that I have a toddler, isn't it?)

▶ **Plan your splurges.** Yes, I know I'm taking a bit of the fun out of it. That's just what I do. Splurge once per quarter (every three months). And better yet, plan your splurges by reducing spending in other categories leading up to the big splurge.

▶ **Don't be a fool.** Yep, that's the type of hard-hitting advice you can only get from Pete the Planner. Splurging on a car is a bad idea. Splurging on a time-share is a bad idea. Splurge on dinner. Splurge on a sweater. Splurge on a gift for your significant other.

Life isn't all about restriction. Your ability to splurge responsibly will serve you well. Yes, planning your splurge is the right thing to do. Don't make this the worst advice I have ever given; please splurge responsibly.

CHAPTER 4

THE PIE: BUDGETING

You've been an adult for more than 30 years. If you're like most people, you've had an on-again, off-again relationship with budgeting. I get it. Budgeting isn't always fun, but it *is* always practical. Given a finite amount of resources, budgeting allows you to prioritize expenditures and make sure that each month-end gives the next month-beginning a chance to succeed. If budgeting has been part of your life on a sincere level over the last 30 years, then you've no doubt felt the impact of resourcefulness and discipline.

Budgeting is complicated in your fifties because of the great exhale that can come with children becoming financially independent, you paying off your house, or even you drinking in the fruits of your income in your prime earning years. Your cash flow may be in the best position it's been in for years. In fact, you may mistake your potentially newfound positive cash flow as budget mastery. It's not.

Because of your fresh breathing room, you might think you are now permanently immune to cash-flow issues. Believe me, once your income transfers from an active (working) income to a passive (not-working) income, your subjective take on budgeting immunity will become instantly ridiculous. You are unlikely to get significant raises to your retirement income the way you may have gotten significant raises during your working career. This reason, more than any other, is why budgeting in your fifties must become a priority.

You likely have no more than 10 to 15 years left in your career, 20 at the most. This means you have no more than 10 to 15 years left of earned income. This earned income must eliminate your debts, fund your present lifestyle, and fund your life post-work. If nothing else, your money life in your fifties needs focus. I hate to be the bearer of good news, but your focus will come in the form of a pie chart. Yep, your budget.

You've heard the term *financial independence* several times. But it's unlikely you've considered, or even heard of, *income independence*. Income independence is the idea and practice of eliminating your monthly financial obligations in order to become less dependent on your income. For instance, if you consistently save 30 percent of your income, gross or net, then you're consistently dependent on only 70 percent of your income. If you save 0 percent of your income, then you are desperately dependent on 100 percent of your income. Don't dismiss this idea as simplistic. It isn't. Well, it kinda is. Yes, it is. Why should retirement planning be any more complicated than that?

Your budget is the key to not only sorting out the complicated nature of your current life, but also allowing you to retire with grace and a confident aura of income independence.

It seems like you should naturally know how to budget. You calculate your income, determine your spending on various expense categories, and then try to spend less than your income provides. But it's just not that simple. Budgeting isn't organic. Budgeting doesn't spontaneously occur. It's a challenging activity that doesn't happen until you decide that it needs to be an important part of your financial life.

And you will eventually get to this point. You will eventually decide that having a budget will enhance your financial life. You can put off this decision for as long as you like, but you will, in the end, budget. A day doesn't go by that a new retiree isn't forced to budget for the first time. Fixed income and fixed expenses always force this decision. When you operate as an adult without a budget for roughly 40 years, being forced to budget becomes a matter of financial survival.

Your income isn't guaranteed to increase, especially once you retire. Your subliminal excuse for not budgeting is bogus. You must budget. But this is where things get tricky. The word "budget" is used to describe several different types of activities and processes. Let's examine these.

- ▶ **Budget (noun).** This word isn't as straightforward as you think. "Budget" can be used to describe antici-pated spending, or it can be used to describe a compar-ison of your income and expenses. The difference often stops people before they get started. My first "budget" was a single snapshot of my expected expenses. But it stopped there. Stopping at the one-time snapshot is a very common yet troublesome mistake.

- ▶ **Budget (verb).** The actual possession or completion of a budget is not sufficient. To actually accomplish some-thing, you must actively budget. Consistent attention to budgeting will lead to lifelong financial success. This isn't as tedious as it may seem. If you are willing to dedicate 20 minutes per month to your finances, then you have a chance of living relatively stress-free.

THE IDEAL HOUSEHOLD BUDGET

The most frequently asked question I get about budgeting is, "How much money should I be spending on each expense category?" Good news: I have an answer for that. It's called the *ideal household budget*.

Don't panic if your expenses don't look exactly like this chart. The key to this entire exercise is to make sure your pie actually equals 100 percent. Yes, in doing this you may find that you spend more money than you make, but we will fix that problem by the end of this book.

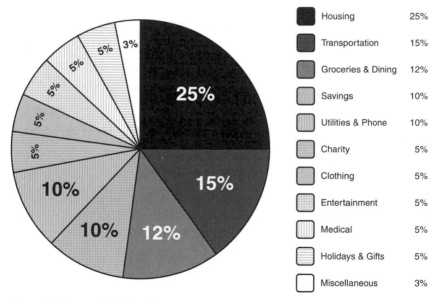

Housing	25%
Transportation	15%
Groceries & Dining	12%
Savings	10%
Utilities & Phone	10%
Charity	5%
Clothing	5%
Entertainment	5%
Medical	5%
Holidays & Gifts	5%
Miscellaneous	3%

The ideal household budget.

Here is what you need to know: If you don't spend the maximum amount in one category, you can allocate more money to another category. In other words, let's say that your household transportation costs are only 5 percent of your income. Then you can feel comfortable allocating the "extra" 10 percent to other categories. This strategy is exactly how I live the financial life I want to live. I have very low transportation costs; therefore, dining out and-housing receive a higher portion of my income. In addition, I don't spend much on entertainment or medical care; therefore, I'm able to utilize these allocations elsewhere. See? It's kind of fun.

People who fail to operate on this give-and-take basis often find themselves in debt. Many households operate on 110 percent of their income. You just can't do that. You can't consistently spend more than you make and expect to come out on the other end. I encourage you to compare your household expenditures to this chart and this philosophy. What one category do you scrimp on so that you can spend more on another?

You'll notice the ideal household budget excludes employer-sponsored retirement plan deposits, such as a 401(k). There's a simple explanation for that. Employer-sponsored retirement plan deposits are often taken out of your income prior to it being considered take-home pay. Thus, if you save 15 percent of your gross income toward your 401(k) and another 10 percent of your take-home pay toward general savings, you are a rock star. Check that—a rock star probably wouldn't save any money.

RENT/MORTGAGE, INCLUDING PROPERTY TAXES AND PROPERTY INSURANCE: 25 PERCENT

Your housing expense is generally your largest one. This means that poor decisions with regard to housing can have a long-lasting impact on your financial life.

Banks have traditionally allowed mortgage payments to approach 33 percent of a gross monthly income (before taxes). That's not at all surprising; a bank is in business to make money first and help you second (or third...or fourth...don't get me started). Thirty-three percent of gross is very different from 25 percent of net. For instance, if your household income is $70,000, 33 percent of your gross monthly income would be $1,924 ($70,000 / 12 = $5,833, and $5,833 × 33% = $1,924). In contrast, 25 percent of your net income on $70,000 would be approximately $1,020, based on $49,000 take-home pay ($70,000 × 70% (30% for taxes and benefits) = $49,000, and $49,000 / 12 = $4,083. $4,083 × 25% = $1,020). That is a difference of $904 per month! I don't know about you, but I spend my net income, not my gross income.

You immediately back yourself into a corner when you commit too much of your income to housing. Based on where you live geographically, it may be easier to keep your housing spending in check. But even if you live in an expensive area for housing, such as San Francisco or Manhattan, knowing your limits is key.

A working person can easily justify putting 25 percent of his or her net pay (take-home pay) toward housing. This figure doesn't include utility costs; it simply accounts for either mortgage (with taxes and insurance) or rent. Can you really justify ending your work income when one category of spending occupies such a significant part of your life? I don't think so. Consider this: If you have a net monthly household income of $4,000 prior to retirement and a $1,000 house payment, then your housing expense equals 25 percent of your take-home pay, as it should. But if your income dips to $3,400/month in retirement, then 29 percent of your income is required to make your house payment. Technically, this forces you to reduce spending in other areas of your life.

TRANSPORTATION: 15 PERCENT

Do you drive your car? Or does your car drive you…to financial trouble? If you're fortunate enough to live in an area with good public transportation, then you're lucky, and you're likely to spend much less on transportation than those people who are forced to rely on personal transportation options.

For the rest of us, getting to the places we need to go costs money. Historically, Americans have moved farther and farther away from our places of employment and have consistently increased the length of our car loans. You might not think so, but living 20 miles away from your job with an eight-year car loan could lead to your financial ruin.

I once encountered a woman who spent 54 percent of her income on transportation. She was in a rough financial situation excluding transportation, and when you threw transportation into the mix, her financial life was a disaster. She spent a majority of the money she earned just to get to her job. She finally relented, gave up being a car owner for eight months, took the bus, and got her financial life back in order.

Car lending has some of the loosest restrictions in the debt marketplace. And allowing a lender or car dealer to dictate the affordability of a certain vehicle will lead to major financial problems.

Transportation costs typically include car payments (leases or loans), gas, insurance, and maintenance. It is very easy to let your transportation costs creep above 15 percent of your take-home pay. This should lead you to one conclusion: You need to find a semi-permanent solution to high transportation costs. Pay off your car and settle close to your place of employment. Based on that hypothetical $70,000 income, you should allocate no more than $612 per month to transportation.

You will find significant savings in the transportation category in retirement, when you get there. Most retirees drive less than they did during their working years, and ideally you will have eliminated your car payment.

Additionally, many retired couples choose to simplify their transportation costs even more by owning only one car. It's not everyone, but owning one car is both cost effective and potentially efficient, based on your lifestyle.

GROCERIES AND DINING OUT: 12 PERCENT

Humans have an odd relationship with food, so much so that we often express our love of food with one of our most precious resources—money. Your money and your consumption of food can at times be overwhelming. I've seen typical families spend upwards of $1,800 per month on food. I've seen financial lives ruined by food, and I once saw a couple blow through 12 percent of their retirement assets in the first year of retirement because they spent so much money on food.

So what is a person supposed to spend on food? And at what point does your food-spending equal a problem?

According to the ideal household budget, it is reasonable to spend 12 percent of your net (after-tax) household income on food. That number includes groceries, dining out, coffee, fermented beverages, and anything else your mouth might consume. For instance, if your take-home pay is $4,000 per month, then your food budget is $480 per month. Is that reasonable? Maybe. But honestly, the 12 percent is a guide. If you spend more than 12 percent of your income on food, then you need to rob some other area of your life to pay for it. What's it gonna be? Your transportation budget? Your savings? Your clothing budget? I don't really care what other area of your financial life you choose to short, but you must account for each and every percentage point that climbs over 12 percent.

People overindulge with food for one of three reasons. First, there's convenience. Any time you exchange money for time, that's convenience. If you are driving home from work and you don't want to take the time to make dinner when you get home, then you must exchange money for convenience.

The second reason people struggle with their food budget is because some people view food and beverage as entertainment. For transparency's sake, this is me. While I sometimes spend too much money on food because of a desire for convenience, I often find that my food overspending is a product of my desire to be entertained by food. I find a delicious meal prepared by a trained chef to be as entertaining as a concert or a movie. And this is specifically why I move the 5 percent that's allocated to entertainment in my ideal household budget toward food. In other words, I spend 17 percent of my income on food. I obviously surpass the prescribed 12 percent, but I account for this by eliminating my entertainment. Besides, I have two toddlers. Entertainment for me is silence.

The third reason people overspend on food is a bit more intricate. I've found that some people are so health conscious that they will buy only organic and specialty foods. While focusing on a healthy lifestyle is certainly a brilliant idea, destroying your finances in the process is a terrible idea. This is why people with a health-food issue should reallocate the 5 percent that's designated for health and medical in the ideal household budget toward food. But if a person with a health-food overspending issue also has other medical expenses, then more expense categories will need to be reduced. Sometimes our health issues require us to spend more money on food. If this is the case for you, just make sure you find the extra money you need to spend on food somewhere else in your budget.

We want it all. The real problems I see often involve people who want convenience, gourmet food, and the healthiest ingredients on the planet. Idealistically, good for them. Realistically, they are going to have a major financial issue that spans years. Food, although a huge part of our lives and culture, is fleeting. We consume it. It leaves our bodies. And as crass as that might seem, your money might just turn into waste.

SAVINGS: 10 PERCENT

Not only should you save money in a company-sponsored retirement plan prior to your paycheck hitting your checking account, but you should also save 10 percent of your take-home pay. This isn't hard to do if you build the habit from your first paycheck. But the further away you get from your first paycheck, the harder it gets. And if you're in your fifties, there's a solid chance you are pretty far away from your first paycheck.

Consistently save 10 percent of your income until your emergency fund (three months' worth of expenses) is full, and then start putting your 10 percent savings toward your middle bucket. We'll discuss the middle bucket at length in Chapter 7, "The Piggy Bank: Saving and Investing."

If you have consumer debt, then the 10 percent allocated to savings should actually go toward debt reduction. From a net-worth perspective, which you'll learn more about in Chapter 7, paying down debt and saving money are the same things. Don't feel pressure to put money in your emergency fund while you're focusing on paying off debt. You can get away with $1,000 or so in your emergency fund while you aggressively attack credit card debt and the like.

UTILITIES: 10 PERCENT

Utilities are utilities, but that doesn't mean you can't help yourself out when making important spending decisions. Internet access, smartphones, and data plans have changed the boring world of utility bills forever. Our addictions to these new types of utility payments have channeled money away from our savings and investments. Anecdotally, it's not uncommon for people to pay more for their smartphone data plan than they save for their child's education.

But it's not just the newfangled utility bills that challenge. Our utility bills don't just happen to us; we sign up for them. Often, our utility costs become more than we want them to be when we buy too much house—the side effect of buying too much house is high utility bills. If you made your housing decision during a string of thriving months and have now come back down to a more modest income level, then not only will your mortgage payment continue to be difficult, but the utility payments that support your home will be difficult, too.

As your family dynamic changes, so will your utility bills. That's primarily because of the number of people using smartphone data plans in your household. I get it. I know that we're all tethered to our smartphones. But again, if you're going to spend upwards of $200 per month on smartphone usage, then you must sacrifice some other habit to the tune of $2,400 or more per year.

CHARITY: 5 PERCENT

Your community will only be as good as your commitment to it. If all of your financial resources are used for your household alone, your community will suffer. When your community suffers, you will suffer. Including charity in a budget is difficult for anyone, but it is important for everyone.

Who said charity costs money? A charitable spirit starts in your mind, not in your wallet. If you are waiting to have money before you give, then you will never give. Money is not the determining factor for whether you give; your charitable spirit is. Volunteer, start a canned-food drive, or give stuff you don't use to a charitable organization. Don't just sit there and do nothing.

It's not unusual to see a pre-retiree's charitable contributions increase prior to and during retirement. With age comes perspective. Sensing and then acting on the needs of your community has an immeasurable impact. You want to feel like you have enough money? Give some of it away. However, money isn't the only resource you have available as a pre-retiree; you also have time. You can reasonably and sensibly replace your monetary contributions with volunteerism if a monetary contribution isn't prudent.

CLOTHING: 5 PERCENT

What's included in the clothing budget? Everything. Clothes for you. Clothes for your spouse. Workout clothes. Work clothes. Casual clothes. Dry cleaning. Clothing repairs. Shoes. Handbags. More shoes.

You may have been excited by the raw numbers, but the "what's included" section may have brought you back to earth. This requires planning and forethought. The first step, in my opinion? You *must* take care of your current clothing.

The bottom line is that you should plan your clothing purchases. If you need to spend more than 5 percent of your take-home pay, that's fine. Just spend less in some other budget category.

MEDICAL: 5 PERCENT

If your health-insurance premiums are deducted from the paycheck you receive from your employer pre-tax, then the 5 percent allocated to medical expenses in the ideal household budget will likely be limited to co-pays, prescription-drug costs, and fitness memberships. If you pay for your health insurance *with* your take-home pay, then this 5 percent allocation must be used for your health-insurance premiums, too. In fact, it's unlikely you'll be able to jam your health-care expenses into 5 percent of your take-home pay if that's the case.

Additionally, as we'll discuss in Chapter 8, "The Pitfalls: Insurance," feel free to pump your Health Savings Account (HSA) full of money. It's a way to defer more money for retirement health expenses and retirement itself. A couple can put well over $7,000 into their HSA each year, which strategically can be used for retirement, once the age of 65 is achieved.

ENTERTAINMENT: 5 PERCENT

Not to suggest that enjoying life isn't important, because it is, but your entertainment expense category should truly form itself around your financial life. If money is tight, stability is nowhere to be found, and ends aren't meeting, then you really shouldn't be spending much money on entertaining yourself— or your young adult children, for that matter. But as we discussed earlier in this book, if your cash flow improves, feel free to use some of that money to enjoy life, once retirement plan contributions are made.

The entertainment expense category includes travel, hobbies, or any other expense that is pleasure-driven. Again, the absence of pleasure isn't the goal; the goal is satisfaction. And satisfaction is deeper than the shallow ilk of pleasure-driven instant gratification.

HOLIDAYS AND GIFTS: 5 PERCENT

Do you want to waste opportunity wrapped in a bow? Blow through your entire margin during the holidays. It happens all the time. The timing of your end-of-the-year bonus isn't a Christmas miracle; it's an arbitrary coincidence created thousands of years ago when humanity needed a calendar. It's easy to trick yourself into thinking that when you're spending money on someone else, it's a justifiable, benevolent decision. It may be, but that's unlikely. If you're spending money on gifts for your immediate family, you're spending money on yourself.

MISCELLANEOUS: 3 PERCENT

The dreaded, mysterious, and foggy miscellaneous spending category can ruin your financial life. Why? Because these are your whims. This is discretionary beyond discretion. You will have miscellaneous expenses, but disorganized, unaccountable people tend to have a ton of miscellaneous expenses.

There are some very legitimate expenses in this category that many reasonable and responsible people will have. The miscellaneous category is your home for life-insurance premiums, disability-insurance premiums, pet expenses, and household items. But if you have a "stop at Target or Walmart on the way home every day" problem, not only will your entire budget suffer, but your miscellaneous budget will also get destroyed.

THE EXPENSE CATEGORIES YOU DON'T SEE

You probably noticed that some very common expenses weren't part of the ideal household budget. Well, lots of expenses aren't part of the ideal household budget. That's not only okay, it's on purpose. Everyone has expenses that don't fall neatly into line with this pie chart. Your challenge is to make room for these other expenses by reducing your spending in the main categories.

As silly as this is to both write and hear, you shouldn't spend more than 100 percent of your take-home pay. However, it's easier said than done. There are many reasons for this, but spending one's gross income is among the biggest culprits. I've found that people often view their income pre-tax and spend it accordingly. For instance, "I make $100,000 per year; of course I can afford a $500 per month car payment." But our gross incomes have very little to do with our net incomes. Based on the amount of deductions you may have, your take-home (net) pay may be only $4,000 per month—not the $8,333.33 per month that we often convince ourselves $100,000 per year gross generates.

EDUCATION

Think back 30 years. Think about how parents of college students were dealing with their children's educational costs. Were these obligations significant? By most measures, no. In the last 20 years, the cost of a college education has skyrocketed. If you've had a child attend college during this timeframe, then you are undoubtedly feeling the effect of this trend in one way, shape, or form. If you've had a student pass through the halls of higher ed in the last 10 years, then chances are your student's college education has greatly impacted your retirement.

Making something like education a priority is great, but making something a priority means de-prioritizing other areas of one's life. If education is going to require more of your discretionary income than the other areas of your life, then you must compromise in the areas you valued greatly in the past. You can't all of a sudden spend more money on education without adjusting the rest of your budget. Sadly, I see this happen quite frequently.

Educations, especially college educations, can be funded via cash flow, with debt, or with assets. If you choose to fund education through cash flow, then just make sure you are adjusting the rest of your budget. If you don't, what you thought was cash flow will quickly turn to debt creation.

DEBT REDUCTION

Ask 100 people how they're going to find enough money to get out of debt, and 99 of them will look outside of their budget. Fortunately, you don't have to look outside of your budget. Your opportunity to pay down your debt lives within your budget. If you have debt—especially consumer debt, such as credit cards, medical bills, or home equity lines—then you need to budget in debt reduction. You must make your debt payments, including additional money to pay toward the principal of your lowest-balance debt, part of your household budget. Debt gets paid off when you take it seriously and stop addressing it with whatever's left at the end of your month.

Look at the ideal household budget and commit to spending less on the core expense categories so that you can rid yourself of consumer debt for good.

VACATION

A vacation is a nice way to reset the stress meter, but going on vacation when you financially shouldn't will only cause the stress meter to spin out of control.

There are a few no-nos when it comes to paying for a vacation. First, don't use a credit card to buy your plane tickets and book your hotel room six months out from a vacation, and then try to figure out how you're going to truly afford it. Pre-fund your vacation, but don't do it with a credit card. Secondly, don't use your emergency fund for a vacation. An emergency fund is not a vacation fund. A $5,000 European vacation is not an emergency, no matter how much you want it to be.

If you have children, vacation decisions get a bit murky with the pressures to create memories and experiences for your children. Family experiences and trips are important, but they must be reconciled with financial reality. Putting your family at a significant economic disadvantage under the guise of memory creation doesn't make much sense.

LONG-TERM CARE

One of the best ways to protect your retirement assets is to purchase long-term care insurance. Long-term care insurance—or LTC, as it's commonly called—helps pay for assisted living expenses in the event that your health fails. It can cost upwards of $200 per day to care for someone in a long-term care facility. If you don't have protection via a long-term care insurance policy, then you must use your retirement assets to pay for your care.

This situation instantly becomes a problem for several reasons. Most importantly, if your income and assets are going to pay for your expensive care, then your spouse's financial needs go unanswered. Long-term care insurance prevents this from happening: Your assets aren't the primary source of funding for your medical expenses when you have LTC coverage.

You need to have a thorough discussion with your financial advisor about how a long-term care stay would affect your financial situation. Long-term care insurance ranges in price, but you should budget in a few hundred dollars per month if you purchase in your fifties. And by the way, you should purchase the policy in your fifties. The younger you are, the cheaper it is.

KIDS

If you become a parent, you find out very early that your financial life will never be the same. From diapers to formula to gymnastics classes, raising a child is very expensive. And as you might know, sometimes it's hard to stop trying to help your kids, even when they are adults. But you make your financial life harder and you make your children more dependent on you when you financially support them as adults.

At least once per year, you should take the time to evaluate how much money you spend on your adult children. Unless there is a unique circumstance that precludes your adult child from working, you should not be actively involved in his or her finances.

One of the biggest expenses that could be on the horizon for you is a wedding. Not yours. Well, maybe yours. But I was initially meaning your children's weddings. If the costs associated with a wedding are on the horizon for you, make sure you set a budget. Don't adopt the "you can't put a price tag on a good time" mentality.

BUT I DO ALL MY SHOPPING AT ONE STORE

Big-box stores have created some interesting challenges for today's consumers. Target, Walmart, Meijer, and the like are great stores that make shopping convenient and nearly effortless. Who doesn't love buying eggs at the same store where you can buy a shotgun or an espresso maker (in Clementine orange)? In other words, you can buy any miscellaneous item with great ease. But when it comes to budgeting, miscellaneous is the bane of human existence. The more miscellaneous expenditures you have, the more challenging budgeting becomes.

And if you think these purchase-all-things-you-could-possibly-need stores are challenging to budget for, consider the problems that warehouse stores such as Sam's Club and Costco can create. How can a person rectify a budget when faced with six months' worth of salad dressing? Well, it's tough. But you must account for the changes in retailers' business practices.

Ultimately, you can adjust your budgeting and financial practices to match the changing nature of your buying habits. For instance, consider making your favorite store its own budget category. Do you have a Target problem? Then make Target its own expense category. This category will most likely engulf your grocery budget, clothing, and even part of your holidays and gifts budget. But that's okay. Budgeting can be more effective when you take your buying habits into consideration when creating your budget categories.

You've heard stories (perhaps even from yourself) of entering one of these types of stores for only one item and ending up with $75 worth of stuff in the cart. How does that happen? Why does that happen? Lots of reasons, but it's less of a big deal when you make the store its own budget category.

Let's say you budget $400 per month for Walmart. Your goal should be to know your limits every time you walk into the store. If you go to Walmart twice per week, then just know you should keep your spending to $50 per trip to stay under your $400 monthly budget. If you go to the store that frequently, then you will know what $50 worth of stuff in your cart looks like.

This is exactly why I go to the same grocery store every week. The more stores you go to on a random basis to get the same type of stuff, the more money you will spend. Being a creature of habit can have its advantages, and one of these advantages is having cart awareness. I don't know about you, but I can look down in my grocery cart and guess the cost of all the groceries within five bucks or so.

The alternative, you ask? The alternative is taking home every receipt, breaking down each item into each budget category, and subsequently ripping all of your hair out as you abandon budgeting forever. My goal for you is to prevent you from giving up on budgeting out of frustration and tediousness. Making your favorite store a budget category will prevent this from happening.

HOW DO YOUR EXPENSES STACK UP?

It's time to put pen to paper. Now that you know what an ideal household budget looks like, you need to take a moment to see how your spending compares. It might be pretty or it might be ugly. Either way, you need to do it.

If your expenses look great next to the ideal household budget, use this opportunity to push yourself even further toward financial wellness. If your expenses look terrible next to the ideal household budget, don't bury your head in the sand and ignore reality.

Your goal in either instance is to identify a chunk of money that you can consistently commit to your financial priorities every month. Chapter 9, "The Plan," will give you the exact action plan for when and how to use this chunk of money. Your goal is just to find it for now.

CHAPTER 5

THE POSSESSIONS: MAJOR PURCHASES

This decade of your life, your fifties, can bring significant expenses associated with big purchases. Sure, there are the major purchases you're used to, such as houses and cars. But your fifties may also bring expenses such as college educations and weddings. Your fifties can cost you a lot of money.

There are day-to-day financial decisions, and then there are huge financial decisions. Huge financial decisions often go hand in hand with huge items, such as houses or cars. Knowing how to best make purchase decisions on huge items will serve you well, not just in your working years but in retirement as well. Often with major purchases come major monthly payment obligations. These payment obligations are what make living on a passive income in retirement so difficult.

Simply put, by eliminating your payment obligations by paying off your purchases prior to retirement, you eliminate the need for income that would be used to offset the obligation. In this chapter, we will examine the proper way to make major purchases and how to prevent yourself from obligating your income to a purchase for longer than you should.

HOUSING

A house is the biggest purchase most people will ever make. Purchasing a house often commits people to paying hundreds of thousands of dollars for the home and tens of thousands (if not hundreds of thousands) of dollars in interest. And it takes three decades to do it!

Being able to keep a housing purchase in its proper perspective is vital to your financial success. If the success of your retirement is based on your ability to balance your available income with your financial obligations, then you must start by examining what is likely your largest financial obligation: your mortgage. If you are a homeowner, then reducing this financial obligation when you're heading into retirement is paramount to your financial success.

Unfortunately, that's not a popular choice anymore. Don't confuse the issue: Pre-retirees would prefer not to have a mortgage expense in retirement, but most often their actions speak louder than their wishes. A 30-year mortgage entered into at age 55 doesn't exactly show a commitment to being mortgage-free at retirement. Sure, there are people who greatly expedite the payoff of a 30-year mortgage to rid themselves of the obligation heading into retirement, yet the reality is that most people who get themselves into a 30-year mortgage at age 55 have no semblance of a plan to pay it off prior to the 30-year note's maturity.

Take a moment and evaluate the role your home plays in your financial life. As a pre-retiree or retiree, does your home currently cause you stress? If so, that stress is unlikely to be alleviated in retirement, unless paying off the mortgage prior to retirement is part of your plan. Ideally, you shouldn't have a mortgage payment in retirement. The interesting thing about this statement is that three decades ago, it wouldn't have been as shocking to read. Today's financing culture has us financing things for longer and at greater amounts than ever before. Just because mortgage lending has loosened to allow you to borrow money for housing during retirement, that doesn't mean you should borrow money for housing during retirement. Even if your home is paid off in retirement, you will still have property taxes and homeowners insurance obligations every single year. Depending on a number of factors, this obligation will still cost you several thousand dollars per year.

YOUR MONTHLY COMMITMENT

Our natural inclination is to buy as much house as we are allowed, and sadly, that natural inclination is disgustingly cruel. In many ways, it's much like eating at an all-you-can-eat buffet. The foolish part of our bodies, wherever it may be, convinces us that more is better. But it's not. More can be hell. I'd argue that "more is better" has become the American Way. Oddly enough, I believe that more is better, just not in the way you'd think.

What do you want more of? This is an essential question, especially for prospective homeowners. Prospective homeowners generally are thinking about housing when they set out to buy a house. But it's foolish for that to be all they think about. Buying a house is a tremendously big deal. In many instances, it's the single largest purchase you will ever make. Yet it's rarely treated that way. It's quite strange how we got here, but somewhere along the way, our homes became disproportionately important to us.

I probably don't need to explain why our homes are such an emotional entity, but I will. Our homes are the epicenters of our memories. They keep our children safe; they host meals, parties, prom pictures, and goodbyes. In many ways, our lives wouldn't be complete without a place to host our greatest memories. All of those things can happen anywhere, perhaps for much less than you're currently spending. You will taint your ability to create lovely memories if you make a foolish housing decision. You can prevent this by having the proper focus when making a house decision. That focus? Your life.

Your life isn't about shelter, couches, curtains, square footage, basements, three-car garages, or corner lots. Your life is about everything other than your house: food, vacations, education, family, entertainment, and a ton of other stuff. You cannot afford to do any of these things or indulge any of your interests if your house payment is a disproportionate share of your household budget. Consider these benchmark numbers for housing.

▶ **40 percent or more of household income committed to housing.** Your margin of error is very slim. You are clinically overhoused. You should seek an immediate solution to this problem, especially if you have a car payment, student-loan debt, and/or other consumer debt. It's nearly impossible to save for the future when this much money is going toward your house payment. It is very unlikely that you have a properly funded emergency fund (three months' worth of expenses).

▶ **26 to 39 percent of household income committed to housing.** You listened to the bank, or you followed the advice of a mortgage calculator. You are spending too much on housing, but it's not a fatal error. If you lack a car payment and significant debt, then you should be fine. If you have a car payment or debt, then you are at risk of hating your financial life for a long time.

▸ **25 percent of household income committed to housing.** Life is manageable, fruitful, and comfortable when you can limit your house payment to 25 percent of your income. You can get the best of both worlds: a nice home and a nice payment.

▸ **Less than 25 percent of household income committed to housing.** Do you want everything and are willing to sacrifice a foolish housing decision to get it? Awesome. Then spend less than 25 percent of your household income on a house payment. Travel the world. Dine out. Drive a nice care. Drink copious amounts of good wine. You can do these things when you don't over-commit to ridiculous housing costs.

Furthermore, if your mortgage or rent payment, combined with your transportation costs (car payment, insurance, gas), is more than 55 percent of your household income, then we've officially figured out why your financial life is so difficult right now.

Show restraint when making a housing decision. You'll actually be able to live a life you want to live.

FIVE SIGNS THAT YOU BOUGHT TOO MUCH HOUSE

One of the most common financial problems facing Americans today is owning too much home. And by owning, I mean being in the process of owning. In other words, securing a mortgage for a house in which you can't afford to live. This is a very serious problem. If this happens to be your problem, then you need to address it ASAP, because foreclosure risk is real for those who can't afford the home in which they live.

What sort of problems can be caused by having too much house? Well, lots—high utility costs, high maintenance costs, and high stress levels, to name a few. But low housing liquidity and high foreclosure risks are what would keep me up at night. *Housing liquidity* describes how easy it would be for you to quickly sell your home at an acceptable price. The lower the liquidity, the harder it would be to get rid of your house in an emergency situation (job transfer, budget constraints, and so on). Unfortunately, as you will see, some of the same signs that illuminate the fact that you can't afford your house will also prevent you from selling your house in a prompt manner.

▶ **You have no equity.** How much of your house do you own? Your answer will determine whether you are in a healthy housing situation. Equity, of course, is the amount of ownership you have in something (in this instance, your home). Do you have less than 5 percent ownership of your home? If so, then you are in too much home. What? The market fell and ate up your ownership? Yes, that stinks, but you still are in too much home. Low equity equals home-selling difficulty. Remember our brief discussion about housing liquidity? Home equity can prevent you from having housing liquidity issues. Low equity isn't the end of the world, but fire is falling from the sky if you have low equity combined with one or two of the following signs.

▶ **Your payment is 40 percent of your monthly income.** The maximum amount of your monthly income that should be dedicated to your mortgage payment is 25 percent. It is quite possible that if your mortgage payment ranges up to 30 to 35 percent of your income, you will still be all right. But if 40 percent of your household income goes to pay your mortgage, then you could be in really big trouble. This isn't always the case, but it is often the case. The more you spend on housing, the less you can spend on everything else! This means you most likely can't save money, can't pay off debt, and can't go on vacation. It is quite common for people who have a major debt issue to mistake a problem of having too much house for a debt problem. Having a high housing cost percentage leaves you very little room for error.

▶ **You can't afford to keep up with yard and house maintenance.** Haven't mulched in two years? Can't afford to paint your house? Those are signs that you can't afford the house in which you live. If you have to go into debt to perform the most basic of home maintenance, then you can't afford your home. The worst part is that neglecting upkeep will only make your problem of too much house worse. Your property value will suffer from your lack of attention. This will increase your housing liquidity concerns.

▶ **You have unfurnished rooms.** What's the point of having a room that you don't use? There is a ritzy section of the city in which I live that is famous for having gigantic homes with no furniture. You don't have to have a perfectly decorated home, but there is something incredibly odd about buying a large home and then not having enough cash flow to furnish it. Right?

▶ **You struggle to afford property tax increases.** I believe that it was Henry David Thoreau who once said, "No, I'm not going to pay property taxes." Okay, he may not have said that, but anyway, no one likes paying property taxes. No one. Property taxes will consistently increase either through increased tax rates or increased property values. Not being able to afford this increase is a major sign that you are in trouble.

If you are guilty of at least three of these problems, then you have a serious problem. You should not take it lightly if you can't afford your current home. That stress you are feeling... yeah, it's real. This problem will not solve itself. But acting in haste will only worsen your problem. I do think that you need to get some professionals involved. You should contact a licensed and trusted realtor to give you an estimate of what your home is worth. You need information. Regardless of whether you sell your home, you need to know where you stand. The solution very well may be that you should sell your home. This is a terribly tough decision, but it could save the rest of your financial life.

So, if you aren't going to sell your home, now what? You *must* turn to your budget. Don't know how much you should spend on stuff? Then use the ideal household budget in Chapter 4. If you can't afford your house, then you are likely committing too much of your household income to your mortgage payment. This means you either need to make more money or spend less money. Spoiler alert for the rest of your financial life: Those are always the two options. In some cases you might want to consider getting an additional job. This should help you temporarily increase your income so that you can take another more permanent course of action (such as selling your house).

If you do sell your house, then you are unlikely to have a ton of equity for a down payment on another house. Take this as a sign from God: Don't buy another house. Rent. Renting is not second place; it is one of the smartest financial decisions you can make. The crazy thing is that you can probably rent a house in the same neighborhood in which you currently live for less than what you are paying for your mortgage.

I can't emphasize my final point enough: Time won't solve this problem. Only three things solve the problem of having too much house: spending less money, making more money, or selling your house. And in most instances, you need to do all three. Don't be embarrassed, be empowered. You are about to take control of your out-of-control financial life. And don't forget, I'm here to help.

THE KEY TO HOUSING SUCCESS

There was a time when mortgages were four years long. You agreed to buy a house, you moved in, and then you had four years to pay it off. If that was still the standard today, then many of us would be renting and/or living in much less expensive homes. Stretching out the length of time on a mortgage is the single biggest reason why home-ownership rates skyrocketed through the middle part of the twentieth century. While the 30-year fixed-rate mortgage certainly has become the most common type of mortgage, the 15-year fixed-rate mortgage often makes more sense.

If you do decide that you have one more home purchase in you, make sure you understand the economics of a 15-mortgage versus the economics of a 30-year mortgage.

By their nature, 15-year fixed-rate mortgages will always have a lower interest rate than 30-year fixed-rate mortgages. This is just the way that debt and liquidity work. For instance, if you let your bank borrow your money for six months, via a six-month certificate of deposit (CD), they may only pay you 0.5 percent interest. But if you let them borrow your money for five years, via a five-year CD, then they may pay you 2.5 percent. This is because you will have much less liquidity if you have your money locked up for five years. This liquidity, or lack thereof, is the primary factor for being able to charge a higher interest rate.

Let's look at a 30-year mortgage at 4 percent on a $200,000 loan (no taxes and insurance).

Mortgage Repayment Summary	
Loan amount	$200,000
Interest rate	4%
Mortgage term	30 years
Monthly payment	$954.83
Total of 360 payments	$343,739.01
Total interest paid	$143,739.01
Payoff date	July 2044

As you can clearly see, you will have paid $343,739.01 to pay off a $200,000 loan. You will have paid the bank 72 percent more than you borrowed originally if you complete the entire mortgage. But in exchange for this large amount of interest that you will pay, you will have a relatively low monthly payment. And as you will notice in my next example, the low payment isn't a product of anything other than spreading out your repayment over 30 years.

Now let's look at a 15-year mortgage at 3.25 percent on a $200,000 loan (no taxes and insurance).

Mortgage Repayment Summary	
Loan amount	$200,000
Interest rate	3.25%
Mortgage term	15 years
Monthly payment	$1,405.34
Total of 180 payments	$252,960.76
Total interest paid	$52,960.76
Payoff date	July 2029

As I said before in the CD example, the shorter the period of time that money is borrowed for, the less the rate of interest charged to borrow. So just for having full access to the equity in your home 15 years sooner, you will get a 0.75 percent lower interest rate. But how much less will you pay in interest? Try $90,778.25. That's 63 percent less interest than the 30-year fixed-rate mortgage. However, your payment will be 47 percent higher on a monthly basis.

In my estimation, it comes down to one thing. You guessed it: your budget. If you can afford to be smart, then be smart (15-year mortgage). If you can't afford to be smart, then don't be stupid. Trying to get a 15-year mortgage when the payment would hurt you financially on a monthly basis is one of the most foolish things you can do. You need to be realistic. If you can't afford it, you can't afford it. You don't need liquidity if your cash flow is tight; you need "stretched out" payments.

In a perfect world, when you choose to buy a home, get a 15-year mortgage. Doing this will require you buy less house than you could if you took out a 30-year mortgage, but owning your home outright in just 15 years will give you a leg up on your financial life.

THE IMPORTANCE OF A GOOD REALTOR

I firmly believe in the importance of hiring a competent financial professional to help guide your financial life. This probably doesn't surprise you. What may surprise you is who I think is the most important financial professional in your life. It's not who you think. Consider the choices. Of course there's a financial planner, an insurance agent, an accountant, and even a lawyer. But I believe the most important financial professional in any of our lives is a realtor. A bad realtor can create havoc in your life for 30 years or more, while a great realtor can ensure stress-free living within your financial limits.

Realtors help people make the largest purchase they will ever make and take on more debt than they will ever take on. I don't know about you, but to me, those two factors alone make the realtor the most important financial advisor a person can have. Here's why most people don't feel like I do: I believe a financial advisor's job—whether the advisor is a stockbroker or a realtor—is to help prevent mistakes. There's an old adage in the investment world: The first step in making money is not losing money. A great financial professional will assess the situation, calculate risks, and advise you on what *not* to do. Show me a financial professional that is a "yes man," and I'll show you a worthless financial advisor.

A great realtor will tell you the truth even when you don't want to hear it. Here are the truths that a great realtor will help you hear.

> ▶ **Some properties don't appreciate in value and may actually decrease in value, even during normal market conditions.** This is a tough pill to swallow for a new homebuyer—an excited new homebuyer at that. Some brand-new homes fall in value during normal market conditions. This can create a series of very scary problems. Stagnant or falling home values can be especially troubling for people who force themselves into a low-price home in lieu of being a renter.

▶ **Loan approval is not confirmation that a purchase is objectively affordable.** Determining the affordability of a home has become a tremendously subjective process, as you've just learned. A great financial advisor (a realtor) can prevent loan approval from becoming the catalyst of a financial disaster. But what realtor is going to speak up and potentially speak out of place? A good one. A really good one.

▶ **There is a bad time to buy a home.** This has nothing to do with real estate as an investment. In fact, unless you're willing to sell your home at the drop of a hat, then it's not an investment. Calling something an investment often justifies poor decisions. If there's a right time and place to buy a home, then there's obviously a wrong time and place to buy a home. I want a realtor who sings this song.

Find a great realtor. Without a doubt, the biggest financial issues I've seen in people's financial lives over the last 15 years could have been prevented by a difficult conversation with an honest realtor. When a true professional tells you something you don't want to hear, listen harder. Don't dismiss the truth.

HOME IMPROVEMENTS

You wouldn't be alone if you wanted to make major changes to the house you currently live in. If this is the case, you need a strategy to pay for all of these changes. Whether it's a kitchen remodel, a room addition, or even new carpet, deciding how you are going to fund your project can mean the difference between financial bliss and financial frustration.

Without a doubt, one of the most popular ways to fund a home improvement project is with a home equity line of credit (HELOC). As you learned in Chapter 2, a HELOC draws against the equity of your home. Your home *secures* the loan, which technically makes it a secured loan.

There are some advantages to HELOCs. The interest you pay on the loan is deductible on your taxes. The payments can be relatively low and are often spread out over a 10-year period. And most people love the seemingly instant access to this big pile of cash. The problem is that it isn't exactly cash; it's borrowed money. It's stone-cold, raw debt. I'd rather you not tap into your home equity to buy things. It's only fair that I present a reasonable alternative to home equity loans. In fact, I'm going to suggest something that I personally did for a major home improvement project, which we completed just a few years ago: Save the money for the project. Saving money for a major financial goal is substantially more productive than funding a financial goal with borrowed money. It's the difference between a store credit card and layaway.

Layaway has gotten a weird reputation over the last couple of decades, but why? Layaway employs delayed gratification, while putting a purchase on a credit card employs instant gratification. Which is better? Frankly, delayed gratification is better because instant gratification funded by debt is dangerous. Trust me when I tell you this: I wanted to complete my home improvement project two years before we actually completed it. But we were unwilling to convince ourselves that having it now was more important than exercising financial sensibility.

We should probably look at some numbers. If you were to take out a $15,000 home equity line of credit with a 4.8 percent interest rate, then 10 years' worth of $163/month payments would pay off your debt and cost you $3,742.50 in interest. In this example, you would pay 24.95 percent more for a home improvement project because you didn't have the patience to save money. On the flip side, if you made every effort to pre-fund the home improvement project prior to starting it, you'd eliminate $3,742.50 in interest expenses, develop invaluable saving skills, and avoid 10 years of payments.

Anecdotally, I've found that people tend to exhale after they borrow money. This results in a complete lack of urgency to pay off the debt. They already received the gratification from the purchase, and the "paying for it" portion of the program isn't a lot of fun. However, it won't take anywhere near 10 years to save $15,000. If the rule is that you can't start the project until you save the money, then you will save the money aggressively, efficiently, and quickly.

The next time you think about borrowing money to make a major consumer purchase, consider trusting yourself and the math instead of trusting a payment schedule.

WHAT REALLY ADDS VALUE TO YOUR HOME

The term *home improvement* itself is a sales pitch. Something that is improved must be worth more money, right? I don't know. The operative term that we are dealing with today is *value*. There's personal value and there's resale value. The confusion between the two concepts goes a long way in explaining why people make so many home improvement mistakes. When you are making a home improvement decision, it's important to ask yourself whether more expenses will equal more increased value. There has to be a tipping point, right? There has to be a baseline of some sort. Putting $10,000 into a basement remodel may increase the home's resale value by $10,000, but a $25,000 remodel may only increase the home's resale value by $14,000.

Unfortunately, every situation is different. But you have to have a baseline. You must. Therefore, here is a list, provided by HGTV, of home improvement projects and how much of the expense of the improvement may be recouped by an increase in resale value.

- ▶ Basement or other unfinished space finishing: 50 to 90 percent. Thus, a $30,000 basement improvement would potentially lead to an increased resale value of $15,000 to $27,000.
- ▶ Kitchen remodeling: 70 to 120 percent.
- ▶ Painting: Up to 300 percent.
- ▶ Bathroom addition: 90 to 130 percent.
- ▶ Bathroom remodel: 65 to 120 percent.
- ▶ Window/door replacement: 50 to 90 percent.
- ▶ Deck addition: 65 to 90 percent.

Almost everyone has heard that swimming pool additions add absolutely no resale value and in some cases can decrease property value based on the high cost of maintenance. But did you know that landscaping doesn't add much value either? It may add curb appeal, but it won't add a great deal of resale value.

Both of these things add a great deal of personal value, and if you have the financial resources to fund these purchases, then have at it. But don't assume you'll necessarily see an increase in your property value because of it.

No matter which project you choose, using debt to fund it is not a great idea. Check that: It's a great idea—according to your bank. But then again, tanning is a good idea—according to tanning places. Your house is not a piggy bank! Although you can borrow against it for things that you deem important, you should not do so.

Did I mention that my assertion is now supported by the Great Recession of 2008? The financial meltdown that we are now (arguably) exiting was fueled by homeowners who stripped equity out of their homes. Home improvement projects funded with HELOCs were a bank marketing gimmick gone awry. It was a bad idea then, it's a bad idea now, and it will always be a bad idea. Fund home improvement projects with money you have saved. And by saved, I mean in addition to your emergency fund money (three months of expenses).

But what about sweat equity? Sweat equity is real. Basically, sweat equity is the concept of doing the work yourself and not paying labor costs to finish a home improvement project. If you have the skills, then doing some of the work yourself could really improve your chances of increasing the value of your home in proportion to your expenses. Labor expenses often double the cost of home improvement projects. If you know what you're doing, a $10,000 (with labor) bathroom remodel may cost you only $5,000 if you do the work yourself. This almost guarantees that you will recoup your costs via increased resale value.

However, we now have a potential problem: If you don't have the skills to complete a home improvement project, your attempt to do so could result in big, big trouble. Not only could you ruin something, but you also could break the law, get hurt, and anger your spouse.

The bottom line is pretty simple:

▶ Choose your projects wisely.

▶ Be realistic about how much your home's resale value will actually increase.

▶ Don't go into debt to remodel.

▶ Utilize sweat equity when applicable.

CAR

Among all of the tricky spending categories, you'll find transportation costs. Car payments, car insurance, and gas seem financially innocuous; in reality, they're anything but. There are more ways to mess up your financial life with poor transportation cost decisions than with decisions in almost any other spending category. You can buy the wrong car, pay too much for it, finance it the wrong way, and then pick the wrong company to insure it. All the while, you are trying to keep your final monthly expenditure under the prescribed 15 percent of your monthly take-home pay. A poor car-buying (or leasing) decision can leave you in the lurch for years.

Going over your 15 percent transportation budget can create a major cash-flow crunch that hinders your ability to make financial progress in the other areas of your life. And while it may seem as though it always makes sense to temporarily bite the bullet on a higher monthly payment via a car purchase versus a car lease agreement, often it does not. If you are struggling with other forms of debt or are paying too much for housing, then finding a very inexpensive lease might be the best financial decision. Yes, despite what you've heard, a car lease might actually save the financial day.

A car lease can make sense if you're in a cash-flow crunch. However, it is neither a long-term solution nor a blank check to get whatever type of car you want. Preferably, if you're in a cash-flow crunch, you'll just buy a very cheap car for cash, but sometimes that isn't an option. And while I realize that leasing a car isn't technically *great* personal finance advice, it is very *practical* personal finance advice. And the reality is that if you're in a big cash-flow crunch, then you haven't shown the greatest ability to handle technical personal finance decisions, so some practical real-world advice is warranted.

If you choose to lease, make sure you aggressively clean up your financial life during the term of the lease. If it's a three-year lease, then you've got three years to clean up debt, tighten down spending issues, and build cash reserves. The goal in all of this is to make sure you're not spending more than 15 percent of your income on transportation costs (car payments, fuel, and insurance). Feel free to ignore this advice, but don't come to me when you're upset.

Transportation costs can get especially difficult when you start adding drivers. I've seen families spend in excess of $400 per month on car insurance, because they had so many drivers. More drivers can equal more cars, more insurance, more maintenance costs, and more gas.

BUT REALLY, SHOULD YOU BUY OR LEASE A NEW CAR?

Buying anything new is exciting, but you would be hard pressed to find many things more exciting than buying a new car. Ahh, that new-car smell, that sparkling finish, that crafty finance manager... Huh? You didn't know that the finance director of a car dealership is part of the experience? Well, then, we have a lot to cover.

Buying a car is not like buying a sandwich. (This observation alone is worth the price of this book.) If you happen to be walking by a deli and you get a hunger pang, you'll likely saunter into said shop and buy a sandwich. Your limitations are quite simple: You either have the money to buy the sandwich or you don't. There's no built-in system that helps your sandwich dreams come true. And if there happened to be a guy who sat in a dark office with the sole purpose of making you a sandwich-owner today with a smile and a handshake, you would probably run. (And, yes, I realize you technically could put the sandwich on your credit card, but just pretend that's not the case, so I can keep this example here. I happen to love the image of a weird sandwich-finance guy sitting in a dark room.) Ahem, back to the car...

So what's different about buying a car? Typically, the missing factor in buying a car is your own affordability awareness. When you buy a sandwich, you know whether or not you can afford it. When buying a car, many people genuinely have no clue. And that is only the first mistake. You need to make many decisions before you ever set foot on the lot. These decisions include how much car you can afford (how much the monthly payment will be), how much your down payment will be, and finally, whether you should buy or lease. This last decision will certainly affect your entire budget.

The option to lease a car has met some bad publicity in the financial world: Many experts feel that leasing is inefficient. Generally speaking, I tend to agree. But leasing a car can be a brilliant way to avoid endless payments for a car you don't want to keep for the long term, or to fit a payment into a tight budget. Let's figure out whether you're one of these types of people.

The first decision you need to make is whether to buy or lease. Look at the following descriptions of a typical car lessee and a typical car buyer and decide which one best describes you.

Typical car lessee

▶ Drives relatively few miles (fewer than 15,000 per year).

▶ Consistently wants a new and/or different type of car every few years. (Is this your vice?)

▶ Needs an affordable (low-payment) short-term solution.

▶ Insists on always having the car covered under warranty.

▶ Takes very good care of the vehicle.

Typical car buyer

▶ Drives an average to high amount (15,000 miles or more per year).

▶ Wants to eventually have no car payment.

▶ Has a greater level of patience with an older car.

▶ Doesn't feel the need to always drive a new car.

▶ Prefers to customize the car.

Which category best describes you?

An oversimplified way to approach this is to decide whether you are someone who insists on always driving a new car. If so, you should consider leasing. Frankly, I don't think that anyone needs to always drive a new car, but I'm not going to waste my time trying to convince you that driving a new car doesn't make sense. If your car is your vice, that's your decision.

Leasing is definitely a worthwhile option for some—but before you commit to it, you should ask yourself the kinds of tough questions you now know to ask before making financial decisions. Do you really need to lease? Could the funds be better spent or saved? Is there room in your budget for a lease? If the answer to many of these questions is no and if you are the average person who just needs a reliable set of wheels to go to and fro, you should be buying, not leasing, a car.

YOUR NEXT CAR PURCHASE

Even if you have determined that your car is your vice and that you want to buy rather than lease, this doesn't mean you should go wild; you will still need to make an intelligent decision. Whether you decide to buy with a loan or take a lease-to-buy option, the goal should be to pay for the car as quickly as possible. Stretching out a car loan or committing to a longer lease is a bad idea. Longer contracts mean less flexibility, and less flexibility means that other financial goals don't get the attention they deserve. You might be tempted to spread out your financing to lower your monthly payment, but the real solution is to buy a less expensive car.

The ideal situation is to bypass a car payment altogether by pre-funding the purchase. This might mean buying a used car or a less expensive one, both of which are far better options than the alternatives: getting locked into high monthly payments or buying a car you can't afford. But I do realize that pre-funding isn't always possible. Here's how to make a car-buying decision that won't destroy your entire budget.

To start, don't finance a car for longer than five years (three is ideal). It would be nice to buy a brand-new car, but when you try to fit your transportation costs into your budget, you will probably have to make cuts somewhere. So, consider buying a certified pre-owned car—a relatively new car that is still under warranty from the manufacturer. Buying a certified pre-owned car strikes the right balance of frugality and practicality. Don't focus solely on the affordability of your car payment. (This holds true whether you buy or lease.) Consider all of the costs involved in transportation (gas, maintenance, and insurance).

You should keep your total transportation costs under 15 percent of your net household income, regardless of whether your household needs one or two cars. If your net monthly income is $4,000, your total transportation costs should be no more than $600.

These may seem like severe restrictions, but if you want to spend more on transportation than prescribed, you will need to make the proper changes to your budget. In other words, feel free to spend more, but know you will need to make significant cutbacks in your budget to allow for this.

Let's see how transportation costs affect your current or future driving situation.

What is your net monthly household income?	$
What is 15 percent of your net monthly household income?	$

How do your current transportation costs compare to this number? Let's take a look, starting with monthly costs.

Current car payment	$
Current monthly fuel cost	$
Current monthly insurance cost	$
Total monthly costs	$

Now, your current annual costs.

Maintenance	$
Oil-change costs	$
Tires	$
Car washes	$
Repairs	$
Total maintenance	$
Monthly maintenance (the total above, divided by 12)	$

Do you have to keep your transportation costs below 15 percent to be a financial success? No. But you must be willing to adjust your spending in other areas.

COLLEGE EDUCATION

In the event that you have children in their late teens or early twenties, it's important you understand how college education funding works. It begins with a very basic yet complicated question. Do you believe your child's education to be a purchase or an investment? It's a pretty wild debate, if you ask me. I'd argue that your end of the bargain is a purchase, and anything your child pays for is an investment. Your child will have a return on their investment, and you will gain satisfaction from your purchase.

But whether you like it or not, in the eyes of the federal government, you are at least partially responsible for paying for your adult child's (18 to 23 years old) education. This has long been the case. The Department of Education, college and universities, and the rest of the federal government also need you to know that if students want to borrow money on their own to fund their own education, without the help of their parents, the parents will still likely be required to fund a portion of the education.

As you learned in Chapter 2, the FAFSA (Free Application For Student Aid) often dictates how much money you and your children are going to pay for their education. If your children are to get any aid at all, they must use your financial information on the FAFSA.

In case you're wondering, children can exclude their parents' financial information on the FAFSA, which increases a student's chances for receiving more financial aid, only if the student is emancipated from the parent. What makes an adult child emancipated from the parent? A few things do—among them, having a child of their own, being married, or joining the military. Other than that, if an adult is 23 years or younger, his or her parent's financial information will determine how much college will cost. Students can't ask for student loans without providing their parents' financial information.

Saving for college has become increasingly difficult for American families. There are two primary reasons for this: 1) decreasing financial sensibility, and 2) college price inflation.

College education has become increasingly inefficient. Whereas technology is leveraged in many industries to decrease consumer costs, colleges (for the most part) have refused to pass on the saving to consumers. Not only that, but colleges have been able to take advantage of student loan subsidization and push college costs even higher. Check out this chart from FinAid.org. It shows college inflation compared to general inflation. College inflation is almost double general inflation. That's not cool.

Year	College Inflation	General Inflation	Rate Ratio
1958–1996	7.24%	4.49%	1.61
1977–1986	9.85%	6.72%	1.47
1987–1996	6.68%	3.67%	1.82
1958–2001	6.98%	4.30%	1.62
1979–2001	7.37%	3.96%	1.86
1992–2001	4.77%	2.37%	2.01
1985–2001	6.39%	3.18%	2.01
1958–2005	6.89%	4.15%	1.66
1989–2005	5.94%	2.99%	1.99

Because the U.S. government is guaranteeing student loans, more students can borrow. This in turn means that demand for a college education is high. And competition to attract and retain students is even higher. This leads to some pretty nutty stuff. Why does your college have a climbing wall? Why does your alma mater have dorms nicer than most three-star hotels? All of these amenities cost money. And you are paying for it. Well, student loans are paying for it.

Am I against sending your child to college? Absolutely not. However, I *am* against cost inefficiency. I encourage you to seek out institutions that honor their commitment to their students' financial futures. For instance, some colleges have begun to offer a four-year degree that students can earn in just three years. This reduces student tuition costs by 25 percent. That makes sense to me. Does it make sense to you?

The easiest way to fund college is to fund this goal over time. If you start saving right away, then time becomes your friend. If you wait until your kid is old enough to spell college, then time is your enemy. Here's what I mean:

- ▶ $200 saved per month for 18 years (started the month your child is born) at a hypothetical 8 percent rate of return will give you $97,071.03 by the time college rolls around.

- ▶ $200 saved per month for 12 years (started on your child's sixth birthday) at a hypothetical 8 percent rate of return will give you $49,188.71 by the time college rolls around.

Waiting just six years cuts your college savings *in half!* That's not good, but it's math. Don't fight math, use it. But if you didn't use math when your children were six years old, then you are facing the consequences of your delay.

College financial aid is one of the most misunderstood beasts in finance, from the snout down to the tail. We first must examine why financial aid is given and in what form. One of the most frustrating aspects of this conversation for parents is that the U.S. Department of Education (DoE) has a much different definition of need than parents do, and the DoE's idea is the only idea that matters.

Financial aid means many things. It means student loans, both public and private. It means scholarships. It means grants. And it means a bunch of other random stuff. When you seek aid, you simply are looking for ways to pay for school, ideally in ways that lessen the cost. When the DoE gets involved—and they almost always do—two things are determined: how much you are expected to personally pay and how much you will easily be able to borrow. That leaves out one weird factor: how much you *need* to borrow.

We should start with what you are responsible for. This is called your *Expected Family Contribution* (EFC). I ran some info through an EFC calculator to help illustrate the DoE's perspective. I don't know your particulars, so I ran some random numbers through the calculator.

Here are the numbers I used:

▶ Household income: $75,000

▶ Investments: $50,000

▶ Cash, checking, and savings: $5000

▶ Parents' ages: 45

Based on the estimates above, the fake family I created would be responsible for somewhere between $6,400 and $8,800 per year in college costs. As CollegeData.com notes:

> "Your real cost—also called your net price—includes your EFC, plus any financial need that your college doesn't cover and any financial aid in the form of loans or earnings from work-study. You will have to cover any unmet financial need from your own resources, repay loans, and work the hours required for work-study aid. The real cost of attending a college includes all the dollars you must spend out of your own pocket, either now or later."

All this is to suggest that someone in your house is going to be borrowing a significant amount of money unless your children receive merit-based scholarships or they go to an inexpensive school. You will get some financial aid, but you should be more concerned about covering your EFC. You will most likely fund this with your 529, your current income (when they are in college), and additional borrowing.

Don't wait to start taking your kids' college educations seriously. Reactively funding a college education can send shockwaves through your financial life that can permanently damage your chances for a successful and comfortable retirement.

THE FINAL FACTOR IN MAKING BIG PURCHASES

Whether you're working or you're retired, your income calls the shots. If you have steady, renewable income, then you'll be able to enjoy a long and fruitful retirement. But if your retirement income strategy lacks discipline, you're in trouble.

You know how to budget, and you know how much house and car you can afford; now it's time to understand the income that will be available to you for the rest of your life.

CHAPTER 6

THE PICTURE: INCOME

When you retire, the income directly derived from your work retires, too. Yet your life and the expenses derived from your life live on. To make retirement work, you must source various income streams to replace your work income.

Some of your retirement income streams have already been established for you, such as Social Security retirement and perhaps a pension. But even if you have income streams established, you still need to ensure that the choices you make around those streams are the right decisions. Your challenges aren't just limited to your choices, either.

The tricky part about transitioning from an income that is directly derived from work to an income that is a mélange of account distributions and retirement-system income streams is avoiding overconfidence and willful ignorance. Distribution mistakes, when they're made, don't provide immediate feedback that something's wrong. Instead, the mistake is often detected 10 to 15 years after it is made, leaving the offender helpless and without recourse.

Think about the financial and retirement advertisements you typically see. The main focus is generally how much money a person needs to retire. And while a big chunk of money is certainly needed, the distribution of that money is what truly dictates success. You can focus all you want on accumulating money, but when you turn those assets into income, you'd better make sure you are still paying attention. Your work isn't done when the money is put away for retirement, despite your wishes. Your diligence and discipline in distributing your assets are vital to your financial survival.

THE STREAMS

When you're working, your income stream is singular in nature. Your household income is what you bring home from work. When you stop working full time, you draw against a number of different income sources.

Most retirement income sources can fall under four simple categories: Social Security retirement, pensions, part-time employment income, and personal savings/investments. You must fully understand how these retirement income sources intersect or don't intersect with your life. You may find you have four out of four of these income streams. Then again, you might find you have only one out of four of these income sources. One thing is certain: No matter how many retirement income streams you have available to you, you must know how much money will be available at your target retirement age.

As you learn about the retirement income streams in the coming pages, take your time considering how these will affect your retirement. For some of these income sources, activating the income can be irreversible. It's fair to say that the longer you wait to take your income from your retirement income sources, the more income will be available. The real trick is selecting distribution timing that is conducive to your desired lifestyle, yet also takes your health and longevity into consideration.

SOCIAL SECURITY

Social Security was first established by President Roosevelt in the years before World War II. Originally, it was created as a system of social insurance for citizens, with a focus on unemployment and old age. These days, though, it's alarming to understand how the Social Security Administration actually describes Social Security retirement payments. Consider the following quote, found on the Social Security Administration website (ssa.gov):

> "Today's Social Security is designed for a few specific purposes: To provide for the material needs of individuals and families; to protect aged and disabled persons against the expenses of illnesses that may otherwise use up their savings; to keep families together; and to give children the chance to grow up healthy and secure."

Uh-oh. Did you pick up on the scary part? Social Security is intended to help protect the savings of the "aged" in the event of illness. Yet more than 35 percent of retirees over the age of 65 rely solely on their Social Security payments for retirement income. They have no savings. Every year, millions of Americans ask Social Security to do a job it was never meant to do: to be the sole source of retirement income.

Social Security is a nice complement to the rest of your retirement plan, but it shouldn't be the main player in your retirement plan. If it happens to be the only source of income for you, your benefits aren't likely to be subject to federal income taxes. If you have additional income sources, you are most likely going to have your Social Security benefits taxed at some level.

WHEN SHOULD YOU START TAKING SOCIAL SECURITY PAYMENTS?

There's a tremendous amount of confusion over retirement ages. Depending on where you look or who you ask, 55, 59-1/2, 62, 65, 66, 67, 70, and 70-1/2 are all considered to be the retirement age in America. Your retirement age is whatever you want it to be, but you gain access to your money in varying degrees at the ages listed.

There actually is a technical normal retirement age, according to the Social Security Administration. Your normal retirement age is based on the year you were born. If you were born before 1937, then your normal retirement age is age 65. If you were born after 1960, your normal retirement age is age 67. And if you were born between 1937 and 1960, then your normal retirement age is determined by Table 6.1, from SSA.gov.

While waiting until your normal retirement age will allow you to receive your full retirement benefit, you don't necessarily *need* to wait until then to take your payments. You can elect to receive payments as early as age 62. If you do take payments prior to your normal retirement age, then you will receive a reduced benefit. For example, if your normal retirement age is 66 and you choose to take payments at age 62, then your benefit will be reduced by about 25 percent. There's a calculator at SSA.gov to help you understand how your early benefit election affects your benefit amount.

TABLE 6.1 Full Retirement Age Based on Year of Birth	
Year Born	Retirement Age
1937 or earlier	65
1938	65 & 2m
1939	65 & 4m
1940	65 & 6m
1941	65 & 8m
1942	65 & 10m
1943–1954	66
1955	66 & 2m
1956	66 & 4m
1957	66 & 6m
1958	66 & 8m
1959	66 & 10m
1960 or later	67

Just because you can take your benefit at age 62 doesn't mean you *should* take your benefit at age 62. If you take your benefit early and you are still working (and earning income), then your benefit will be reduced even further. There isn't a magic formula for deciding whether you should take your benefits early, but if you don't need the money, you are in good health, and you'd like to receive a higher payout at your normal retirement age, then wait until your normal retirement age. If your health is in question, you need the money, and you can't wait until your normal retirement age, then take the early retirement payout.

If you wait until age 70 to start drawing Social Security payments, you can increase your monthly payout in excess of 30 percent. A $2,000 monthly payment at 66 can turn into a monthly payment of $2,500 if you wait until age 70. Again, the factors that will affect this decision are your income sources, your health, inflation concerns, and your significant other's age.

HIDDEN BENEFITS?

I get tickled when I hear or read ads that claim to reveal the secrets of Social Security. There aren't any Social Security secrets. People simply don't take the time to know what they should know to better their lives. Just because you don't know the details of something, that doesn't mean you are missing out on secrets. Take, for example, the paper cups you use to hold ketchup at your favorite fast food restaurant. You're probably using them wrong. The tiny white cups are designed to expand when you tug on the accordion-folded walls. Each cup can hold three times more ketchup than you think. Boom. I just changed your life. Details are rarely secrets, but you need to know them to maximize utility.

What's incredibly interesting is that Social Security has an impact on all of our lives while working (via payroll deductions), and Social Security retirement payments are a core retirement income strategy for the majority of Americans, yet the average worker in the prime of his or her career, pre-retirement or even in retirement, doesn't fully understand how the details of the program can enhance his or her financial life.

For instance, many divorcees are surprised to learn that even though their marriage is over, their financial relationship with their ex-spouse is not. In fact, as long as a divorcee is over the age of 62 and hasn't remarried, they can claim Social Security retirement benefits on their ex-spouse's account. The claim can take place if the divorcee isn't currently remarried, even if the ex-spouse is remarried. And whether you like it or not, claiming your ex-spouse's Social Security retirement benefits doesn't negatively impact that ex-spouse.

The prospect of this strategy gets a little more exciting when you discover that you can claim your ex-spouse's Social Security benefits and allow your own Social Security benefits to continue to accrue. You can claim theirs, allow it to positively impact your financial life, and then later receive your Social Security benefits on a more permanent basis. Of course, there are rules. The divorcee must be of full retirement age (somewhere between 65 and 67, depending on what year he or she was born in) to claim his or her ex-spouse's benefit. Don't worry; if your ex-spouse is remarried, his or her current spouse will be able to make a claim on your ex-spouse's account, too.

Among my favorite Social Security retirement strategies, you'll find the ol' "file and suspend." This is very similar to claiming your ex-spouse's benefit when you are at full retirement age, but in this instance, you have to/get to still be married. At full retirement age, one person files for his or her benefits and immediately suspends receiving benefits, and then the spouse makes a spousal claim for 50 percent of the filer's benefit. All the while, the original filer's benefit accrues at a 7 to 8 percent clip per year, and then flows back to the retiree at age 70. This is a great strategy for healthy couples that can afford to delay full retirement benefits. Couples can have their cake and eat it too, in a way.

Spouses can claim Social Security benefits even if they might not be Social Security eligible with their own work record (for example, they had too few qualified work quarters). A spousal benefit is generally available once you reach the age of 62 and the filing spouse is north of 62. The spousal benefit can be equal to 50 percent of the filer's full retirement benefit if the filer filed at full retirement age.

It is worth your time and attention to run numerous scenarios and calculations. Start at SSA.gov. It's an extremely comprehensive website.

PENSION (DEFINED BENEFIT PLAN)

According to a *Time* magazine report, in 1980, 39 percent of private-sector employees had a pension. Yet by 2010, the percentage of people covered by private-sector pensions fell to 15 percent. That's a drop of 62 percent in just 30 years. What has caused this shocking drop off? According to Richard Ippolito and Thomas A. Firey in a 2002 article from National Review

Online, "[It] was the result of well-intended government action gone awry." Tax changes in 1986 and 1990 caused many pension-based retirement plans to call it quits. Enter the 401(k) plan.

Since the inception of the 401(k) in 1980, the popularity and use of defined benefit plans—or pensions, as they are more commonly known—has fallen. The use of 401(k) plans has grown in inverse proportion to the shrinking of employee pensions. If you happen to have a pension, then you are in an increasing minority. Despite the popularity of 401(k)s and their widespread use, the Center for Retirement Research at Boston College reports the median household retirement account balance in 2010 for workers between the ages of 55 and 64 was just $120,000. In other words, the plans are being offered, but employees aren't fully taking advantage of them.

For those with a pension, choosing your pension distribution option may be one of the most important financial choices you are ever forced to make. There are two main decisions to be made, and neither decision is necessarily easy.

▶ If it's an option, should you take a lump-sum payment in lieu of lifetime monthly pension payments?

▶ How should your pension provide for your survivors in the event of your death?

Before you begin to answer these questions, it's important that you take the time to explore how safe your pension is. A pension plan can fail. Some of the biggest companies in the history of the United States have had failed pensions, including United

Airlines, Delphi, and Bethlehem Steel. Luckily, there's some good news...and some bad news. The good news is there's a government entity that insures pensions across the United States. It's called the Pension Benefit Guaranty Corporation (PBGC). It steps in when a pension plan goes splat. The bad news is that even the PBGC is subject to risk. In 2008, the PBGC's funds, which are used to pay pension obligations, lost 23 percent of their value when the PBGC decided to change some of its bond holdings into stock holdings. These losses didn't necessarily affect payouts, but they did cause many to question the long-term viability of the PBGC.

As you make your pension election, you should keep the possibility of pension failure in the back of your mind. It can happen. This shouldn't cause you to panic, but if you have a strong reason to doubt the viability of the pension plan, you should thoroughly discuss your options with your financial advisor.

LUMP-SUM PAYMENT VERSUS LIFETIME MONTHLY PENSION PAYMENTS

Should you take a lump-sum payment in lieu of lifetime monthly pension payments? This is a million-dollar question. No really, sometimes it is. Of all the conversations you have with your financial advisor, this is among the most important. It's a question of risk. Are you willing to take on the risk of managing the lump sum to create your retirement income stream? Or are you more comfortable with your former company's ability to manage your retirement income stream?

It's not easy to stare down the barrel of a several-hundred-thousand-dollar lump-sum payment and decide to take a lifetime monthly income stream instead. But sometimes this is the best option.

Let's examine a very simple, yet realistic scenario. You are faced with two options: Option 1 is to take a lump-sum payment of $800,000. Option 2 is to take lifetime payments of $56,000 per year. Which should you choose? You will learn more about retirement distribution rates here in a moment, but it would take a 7 percent distribution on your lump sum to recreate the $56,000 per year retirement income. Do you believe a 7 percent fixed rate of distribution on your investments to be realistic and/or wise? And what happens if you die? If you choose the annual pension of $56,000, what is your spouse to do when it disappears upon your death? On the other hand, if you take the lump sum, how should you manage it to create a repeatable and reasonable income stream? All of these ideas lead us to the next major question.

I can't make a specific judgment about your ability to handle hundreds of thousands dollars and 168 hours per week to do whatever you want with it, but I can tell you that despite my mastery of financial wellness and investments, I wouldn't fully trust myself with that plethora of resources. Whatever constraints you might fear in regard to a structured retirement payout must be rectified with your personal ability to create your own sound income strategy. This is where many people make gigantic retirement mistakes.

SURVIVOR BENEFITS

If you select the monthly benefit option instead of the lump-sum payment, then you will need to decide how this choice will affect your loved ones, especially your spouse. Most pension plans allow you to elect a smaller monthly benefit to provide a portion of the monthly benefit to your spouse in the event of your death. Can you imagine having a significant amount of your household retirement income ripped away from your spouse when you die? Well, you should imagine it, because if you choose the wrong payout option, then it will be reality.

You can employ various strategies to prevent an income meltdown when you die. If you elect a monthly payment from your pension plan, then consider taking a reduced amount of income up front, in order to provide an income stream to your spouse. Or better yet, elect to take the highest monthly payment possible, and then ensure that your spouse is taken care of by buying the appropriate amount of life insurance to replace the lost benefit upon your death. This strategy allows you to maximize your pension and provide for your spouse. However, there are some additional considerations when employing this strategy, such as insurability and insurance affordability. In addition, if you choose to go this route, make sure you get qualified for life insurance before you make your final pension election. And as always, you should certainly discuss this strategy with your financial advisor. Being able to maximize your pension via the use of life insurance is a brilliant move with very few risks. You just need to be able to qualify for the life insurance, and you must be able to afford the life insurance premium. Neither of these factors should be taken for granted.

SO YOU WANT THE LUMP SUM?

If you do choose to take the lump sum, then it immediately becomes an investment asset. You now take 100 percent responsibility for what happens to it. You take 100 percent of the risk. This isn't to scare you, it's just the truth. When you say no to the monthly pension payout, you are saying yes to your ability to re-create the distribution rate you just declined to accept. That, or you don't need income off the lump sum. If you don't need any income off of your potential lump-sum distribution for quite some time, then taking the lump sum in lieu of the monthly payout may make sense.

If passing on money to future generations is a goal of yours, and you don't necessarily need income from this aspect of your retirement plan, you should almost always take the lump sum. But you need to be realistic in your ability to pass money onto your heirs. I find that people tend to be overconfident in their assets' ability to remain viable not only throughout their lifetime but upon their passing, too.

EMPLOYMENT

You wouldn't be alone if you chose to work part-time during retirement. According to a 2012 report on the Transamerica Retirement Survey, "the majority of workers in their fifties and sixties plan to work after they retire, with 52% reporting that they plan to work part-time and about 9% reporting that they plan to work full-time. Fewer than one in five workers (19 percent) do not plan to work after they retire."

The reasons why people work during retirement vary. Many people work during retirement for health insurance benefits, although the number of people who fail at this strategy outweighs the successful ones tenfold. A poor healthcare strategy is one of the biggest impediments to a successful retirement. Many individuals work during retirement to keep their minds fresh and skills relevant. This reasoning is both legitimate and vital, yet this book isn't the proper forum for that discussion.

From a practical standpoint, employment income at retirement may simply be a necessity. You may need the income as part of your retirement income strategy.

On your quest to create guaranteed renewable income, it's important for you to understand that employment income during retirement is not guaranteed renewable income. Just like most part-time jobs, the part-time jobs that retirees often take are disposable at best. Whereas these jobs might be important, fulfilling, and income-producing, they aren't always reliable. The realistic unreliability of these part-time jobs can cause serious problems for your retirement income plan. Beyond that, it is unrealistic to think that you will physically be able to work for the duration of your retirement.

INCOME DERIVED FROM YOUR INVESTMENTS AND SAVINGS

For a moment, assume the only food source on the planet is chicken. Your only choices for sustenance are eggs or the meat of the chicken. Every day you are faced with an elementary decision when your stomach starts to growl: eat eggs or eat chicken. However, you should know there is a finite number of chickens. There are limitless eggs, as long as there are chickens to produce the eggs. Eat too much chicken, and you'll run out of eggs. Do you see the problem?

Your retirement plan isn't much different. The income you create off your assets (savings, 401(k), mutual funds, stocks, bonds, and so on) can only be created when there is an asset to create it. In other words, eggs can only be created when there are chickens around. If you run out of chickens, you run out of food. If you run out of assets, you run out of income.

Without a doubt, one of the most heinous financial mistakes you can make in retirement is spending large chunks of money—or more specifically, spending more money than you earn in interest on your assets. If you are spending at a faster rate than your assets are earning, then you will undoubtedly go broke. It's worth noting that going broke is bad during retirement. To protect yourself from going broke in retirement due to using your income-producing assets for big purchases, you need to have two types of assets: chunk money and income-producing assets.

Chunk money, which is not a technical term, is money used to fund large expenditures, such as vacations, cars, home repairs, or large medical bills. The role of chunk money is very basic: to prevent you from accelerating the distribution rates of your income-producing assets. You will undoubtedly have expenditures in retirement that require chunks of money. You must set some money aside to deal with these expenses.

On the other hand, income-producing assets are assets designated not to necessarily grow, but to generate a stream of income in retirement. Ideally, this income is produced without cutting into the asset itself. An investment can stick around forever, risk permitting, if you live only off of the interest or income. Having said that, it's preferable that the asset actually grow.

There are several ways in which an investment asset can produce a stream of income.

▶ **Interest.** You are probably the most familiar with this type of income. Your savings account generates a small percentage of interest. Certificates of Deposit (CDs) produce interest, and bonds pay interest. Bond interest may have a huge impact on your retirement planning. Retirement planning uses several types of bonds, including municipal bonds, corporate bonds, and treasury bonds. Your financial advisor will be able to assess the appropriateness of bonds for your particular situation.

▶ **Dividends.** If you own individual stocks or stock mutual funds, you may receive dividends. In short, dividends are your share of the profit of the companies you own. Because as you know, if you own a stock or stock mutual fund, you own part of a company.

▶ **Annuity payments/withdrawals.** Annuities are popular tools for creating guaranteed income in retirement. They typically pay out income via two different methods. Traditionally, an annuity creates income by annuitizing an asset. This means the annuity owner gives up complete rights and control of the asset in order to obtain a guaranteed lifetime income stream from the annuity (insurance) company. More recently, annuity owners have been able to secure a guaranteed income stream from their annuities without surrendering rights to the initial deposit. These types of withdrawals are often called *guaranteed withdrawal* or *guaranteed income riders*.

▶ **Rent.** If your retirement plan includes receiving payments from your rental properties, then your retirement income will be subsidized with rent.

▶ **Liquidation.** This means you will need to sell your investments to create an income stream. You will be cannibalizing the principal. Does that sound ominous? Good, it is. There's no turning back once you dip into the principal. This is why distribution rates are so important.

HOW MUCH INCOME CAN YOUR ASSETS SAFELY PROVIDE?

I recently surveyed hundreds of financial advisors with an average of 14 years of industry experience. Collectively, this group agreed that the proper distribution rate at retirement is 4 percent. Your understanding of this concept is vital to the success of your retirement. To help you understand this idea better, we should head to Monte Carlo.

MONTE CARLO SIMULATION

A 2010 study conducted by Allianz Life Insurance Company of North America indicates that 61 percent of individuals fear running out of money in retirement more than they fear death. It's quite a scary thought. What would happen if you ran out of money? How likely are you to run out of money? Both of these questions are important to explore.

It has been my experience that very few people do the formal calculations that would help them understand whether they are likely to run out of money during retirement. Why? Because it's terrifying. On top of that, they don't know how to figure it out. Most financial advisors should be able to help you with this calculation, yet nearly two-thirds of retirees do not have someone they consider to be their financial advisor (based on a 2011 Life Insurance and Market Research Association International report). Fortunately, there's a very simple tool for figuring out the probability of running out of money over a set period of time given a set withdrawal rate. It's called a Monte Carlo simulation. Sounds like gambling, doesn't it? Well, it's not.

Before you peruse these tables using the Monte Carlo simulation method, you should prepare yourself to see some surprising things. As noted earlier, most seasoned financial advisors prefer an asset distribution rate of 4 percent. Also noted earlier is that only 33 percent of pre-retirees have someone they consider to be their financial advisor. Lack of good advice likely results in people distributing too much money from their nest egg as retirement income. Tables 6.2 through 6.4 will show the results of taking more than the prescribed 4 percent. In recent years, even the 4 percent distribution rate "rule" has been called into question by economists and retirement planning experts due to a sustained low-interest-rate environment. The lower-interest-rate environment of the early 2010s has made it more difficult to have certainty in the permanency of taking 4 percent withdrawals and having your money last long enough.

In a moment, you will see several Monte Carlo simulation tables. Each table represents a different investment style. Each table was created by running more than 5,000 scenarios using various investment indexes' rates of return dating back to 1926. The percentages indicate the number of successful scenarios—successful meaning the simulation didn't result in running out of money. In other words, these tables are thorough and real. One hundred is the best number because it indicates that you have a 100 percent chance of success.

Here's how you read the table. When examining the first Monte Carlo simulation with a 50 percent bond, 30 percent cash, 20 percent stock allocation, you will see that withdrawing 6.5 percent of your portfolio's value every year, over 25 years during your retirement, gives you only an 18 percent chance of not running out of money. That's suggesting you have an 82 percent chance of failure when trying to make a 6.5 percent distribution rate last 25 years. Thus, the higher the number in the table, the more likely you will have a successful retirement. You will need to decide what is an acceptable rate of success and what is an acceptable rate of failure.

The following information and tables may appear to be complicated and intimidating, but they aren't. Take your time as you absorb the Monte Carlo simulation concept to ensure you are making the best decisions for you and your family.

Let's examine this concept even further. If you have $300,000 in retirement assets at the beginning of retirement, a 6.5 percent distribution rate would provide you with an annual income of $19,500. You would then withdraw 6.5 percent of the balance the next year, no matter the balance of the portfolio. Here's the problem: If your portfolio doesn't provide at least a 6.5 percent rate of return on the underlying investments, then you would withdraw more money than the portfolio created that year. This means you'll start eating into the principal balance. Additionally, if your portfolio falls in value, you'll need to withdraw more than 6.5 percent to produce the same dollar amount of retirement income. But if you simply tried to withdraw 6.5 percent of your total portfolio value every year for 25 years, then there's still only an 18 percent chance you'll succeed in doing so. There's an 82 percent chance you'll run out of money along the way. And this accounts for 5,000 different investment performance scenarios that the 50 percent bond, 30 percent cash, and 20 percent stock allocation could create.

As you examine the following tables, match the table that most accurately depicts your investment style as you enter retirement. If you don't know what your investment style is or should be, then we have yet another reason for you to find a great investment advisor.

TABLE 6.2 Monte Carlo Simulation: 50 Percent Bond, 30 Percent Cash, 20 Percent Stock

Percent of Portfolio Used per Year	10 Years	15 Years	20 Years	25 Years	30 Years
3.00%	100%	100%	100%	100%	100%
3.50%	100%	100%	100%	100%	97%
4.00%	100%	100%	99%	97%	89%
4.50%	100%	100%	99%	91%	73%
5.00%	100%	100%	95%	77%	50%
5.50%	100%	100%	88%	57%	30%
6.00%	100%	99%	72%	35%	14%
6.50%	100%	95%	55%	18%	6%
7.00%	100%	88%	34%	8%	2%
7.50%	100%	74%	19%	3%	0%
8.00%	100%	57%	8%	0%	0%
8.50%	100%	39%	3%	0%	0%
9.00%	98%	24%	1%	0%	0%

TABLE 6.3 Monte Carlo Simulation: 60 Percent Stock, 40 Percent Bond

Percent of Portfolio Used per Year	10 Years	15 Years	20 Years	25 Years	30 Years
3.00%	100%	100%	100%	100%	99%
3.50%	100%	100%	100%	98%	96%
4.00%	100%	100%	99%	96%	92%
4.50%	100%	100%	97%	92%	86%
5.00%	100%	100%	94%	85%	79%
5.50%	100%	98%	90%	79%	69%
6.00%	100%	96%	83%	69%	59%
6.50%	100%	92%	75%	60%	48%
7.00%	100%	87%	65%	52%	41%
7.50%	99%	81%	58%	41%	30%
8.00%	98%	74%	47%	32%	23%
8.50%	96%	66%	38%	24%	18%
9.00%	94%	57%	32%	18%	12%

TABLE 6.4 Monte Carlo Simulation: 100 Percent Cash					
Percent of Portfolio Used per Year	**10 Years**	**15 Years**	**20 Years**	**25 Years**	**30 Years**
3.00%	100%	100%	100%	100%	94%
3.50%	100%	100%	100%	97%	65%
4.00%	100%	100%	100%	75%	19%
4.50%	100%	100%	94%	33%	2%
5.00%	100%	100%	73%	6%	0%
5.50%	100%	100%	33%	0%	0%
6.00%	100%	96%	7%	0%	0%
6.50%	100%	81%	1%	0%	0%
7.00%	100%	47%	0%	0%	0%
7.50%	100%	16%	0%	0%	0%
8.00%	100%	3%	0%	0%	0%
8.50%	100%	0%	0%	0%	0%
9.00%	97%	0%	0%	0%	0%

UNDERSTANDING AND MEASURING RISK

Your retirement income plan must be permanent. You cannot, under any circumstances, employ an income plan that leaves you without income as you get older. You need a proper understanding of risk to make sure this doesn't happen.

On some level, risk is necessary. In addition to its necessity, risk is omnipresent. While you may avoid investment risk, you won't be able to avoid inflation risk, interest-rate risk, or liquidity risk. Most people's understanding of risk stops at market risk. The term *market risk* is used to describe the possibility of losing money due to financial market activity. An example would be if you lose money when your favorite stock decreases in price. The risk was that the financial markets acted naturally, and then you were exposed to the possibility of loss. When people are described as *risk-averse*, they are actually market risk–averse. They don't want to expose their money to the possibility of loss due to market activity.

Misjudging market risk is one of the main causes of going broke in retirement. Whether you personally make the misjudgment or your financial advisor makes the misjudgment, if your investments decrease in value, then any income taken on those investments only compounds the problem. This doesn't mean you shouldn't take market risk in retirement; it just means you need to understand truly what is at risk. By the end of this book, you will know exactly how much market risk you need to take. It is wise not to take an ounce of market risk more than necessary to accomplish your retirement goal.

In the Monte Carlo simulations in Tables 6.2 through 6.4, you will notice that each table represents a different investment allocation. And in turn, each allocation represents a different risk tolerance. The more equity positions in your portfolio (stocks), the more risk tolerant you are. While you can certainly see which allocations work best, you shouldn't necessarily adopt the corresponding investment allocation for your own investments. You should always consult your investment advisor when making major changes to your asset allocation. If you've been a pretty balanced investor in the past, a switch to 100 percent stock would be a major shock to the system and could be detrimental to both your short-term and long-term financial health. Tables 6.2 through 6.4 may make you feel like there is one ideal portfolio construction for retirement success, but that isn't the case. Your risk tolerance is very personal. It's your ability to tolerate market fluctuations in your portfolio without freaking out.

If nothing else, the Monte Carlo simulations in Tables 6.2 through 6.4 will help you understand not only the impact your distribution strategy will have, but also your justified unwillingness to take risk with your money. Want to be in 100 percent cash? That's fine, but your actions no longer have mysterious results. The results are very clear and very real.

WANT VERSUS SHOULD

One of the biggest mistakes you can make is to take distributions based on what you want, rather than on what is reasonably available to maintain consistent income throughout your life. You may ask, "But what if I need more income than my assets, pension, and/or Social Security can provide?" Excellent question. Unfortunately, the answer—or better yet, the *answers*—to this question can be bitter pills to swallow. Here are the possible answers to the question:

▶ You can't retire.

▶ You can't retire right now.

▶ You need to reevaluate what you "need."

▶ You need to employ the fourth stream of retirement income: employment.

Your retirement will end in disaster if you bleed your assets too quickly. Don't ignore the risks and the Monte Carlo simulations discussed earlier. Hoping things work out is a terrible strategy. You cannot wing it. Blindly forcing out too much income, or taking whatever you feel like taking, is not the same as driving an extra 50 miles with your fuel light on and hoping for the best. Ignorant perseverance will lead to an irreversible outcome.

PROJECTED INCOME AT RETIREMENT

You understand the different income sources, so now you need to project what will be available for you on your retirement date. Before you do this, though, you will need to project your portfolio's value at your retirement date. The concept of the calculation works like this: Take the current value of your investments, plus any additions you will make over the next few years until retirement, all at a hypothetical rate of return until the day you retire. It's a fairly complicated calculation with several moving pieces. But the most important thing for you to know is that you should not overestimate the rate of return you receive on your investments. I've provided a retirement asset projection calculator for you at PeteThePlanner. com/retirement-calculator.

Once you arrive at a projected investment asset total that corresponds to your retirement-age goal, then you will need to go back to the Monte Carlo simulation tables from earlier in this chapter. Find the table that most closely matches your projected investment style/philosophy at retirement. For instance, if you believe your portfolio will consist of 60 percent stocks and 40 percent bonds, then find the corresponding Monte Carlo simulation table. Now, choose a distribution rate for your income-producing assets. As discussed earlier in the chapter, many investment professionals feel as though 4 percent is the best bet. If you'd like to choose a different distribution rate, that's fine. You just need to be comfortable with the consequences of your selection.

Your process might look like this:

1. Determine that your $400,000 portfolio will grow to $600,000 over the next 10 years given a particular rate of return and the proper additions.

2. Select the Monte Carlo simulation table created using a 60 percent stock and 40 percent bond allocation, if it is indeed your investment style and mix.

3. Select a distribution rate of 4 percent.

4. Confirm that you are comfortable that a 4 percent distribution rate has a 92 percent chance for success over 30 years of distributions.

5. Arrive at $24,000 as your first-year investment income at retirement.

Add this together with the Social Security retirement estimates provided to you by the Social Security Administration, any rental income, and your projected pension amount (at your target retirement age). This is your gross (before taxes) retirement income. Your final totals would look like the numbers below:

$24,000 from investments

$20,000 from Social Security retirement

$0 pension

$0 rent

$44,000 total

A HAPPY ACCIDENT

I have really good news, which I'm really excited to deliver to you. If you are behind the retirement eight ball, so to speak, there is still hope for you. You may have just realized this same thing in the previous section. If you've never taken time to run the numbers, then you may find some surprises when you do finally run the numbers. Your projected income may actually fit your projected expenses by accident.

Yes, you may have accidentally prepared for retirement. Some people are quite diligent when it comes to retirement preparation; others are not. But if you have relatively low expenses, you paid off your mortgage, and you have a pension and Social Security, you may actually be set and ready to go. Don't tell anyone this, but having retirement investments isn't 100 percent essential to a successful retirement.

Don't get me wrong; I want you to have retirement investments. I want you to have them for several reasons. Retirement investments help to wean you off your work income, especially if you invest on a regular basis and consistently increase your contributions. And retirement investments can help mitigate the financial risks associated with financial emergencies. Just because a lack of investing hasn't affected your ability to retire, that doesn't mean you shouldn't invest and save going forward.

If you're in this accidental boat, don't get complacent. Accept the gift that is a happy accident and then push yourself hard as you approach retirement. Your newfound diligence will most certainly pay off.

TIGHT FITS DON'T FIT

It's been my experience that pre-retirees focus in on age 62. And whether 62 is a realistic retirement age or not, it becomes the catalyst of obsessions. This is to say that you may also be randomly focused on age 62. The access to Social Security retirement payments is what makes this age so seemingly appealing. But being able to take Social Security and retire at 62 isn't the same as successfully retiring at 62. Retirement is not the day you stop working, it's a several-decade stage of life.

If you can only barely make retirement work for you at age 62 by tapping all of your different income sources, don't retire. Please know that my intent isn't to rain on your parade; my intent is to make sure your parade lasts longer than three years.

Because of inflation, specifically within the healthcare industry, retirement gets more expensive the longer you are retired. If your budget is just barely balanced on Day 1 of retirement, then Day 2,000 is going to be brutal.

What no one has ever told you is that even when you're retired, retirement is a moving target. Your expenses continue to shift and increase, and your income quickly begins to feel the effects of inflation. Not only is it wise to make sure you can grow into your expenses in retirement by showing a budget surplus early in retirement, but you should also consider planning a strategy that will give you raises throughout retirement.

Raises can come in many forms. For instance, you can start off your retirement by only taking 2 percent distributions and then shift that number closer to 4 percent as retirement progresses. You could also wait a few years, once retired, to begin drawing either Social Security or a pension.

In either instance, you will have learned to live on one level of income prior to making more income available. This income distribution strategy should go hand in hand with your investment strategy. And if you didn't already know this, you need an investment strategy. Which brings us to your investments. It's time to get you up to speed on them.

CHAPTER 7

THE PIGGY BANK: SAVING AND INVESTING

Not to freak you out, but from an investment perspective, there is no decade more important than your fifties. Why? To begin, time is no longer on your side. That $100 you saved when you were 21 years old has had at least 30 years to grow. The $100 you save now has much less time to grow. And the complexities of your investing life don't end with growth time.

Investing in accordance with your risk tolerance is also more important than ever before. Blind investing ignorance in your thirties can sometimes correct itself; in your fifties, it can't. I have seen far too many people ruin their chances at retiring at their preferred retirement age simply because they never took the time to readjust their investment portfolios to match their investment time horizon.

The lack of a financial advisor can lead to many problems as well. A financial advisor is a trained professional who can identify and address the common errors of do-it-yourself investors. We'll discuss relationships with financial advisors more in a bit, but just know they can mean the difference between success and failure.

But ultimately, investing in your fifties can be complex because your attitude may switch from *grow, grow, grow* to *give me income and preserve my money*. Technically, grow, give me income, and preserve my money are called *investment objectives*. Your investment objective for the last 30 years or so has been accumulation. That's about to change.

ACCUMULATION TO DISTRIBUTION

You are extremely close to crossing over the accumulation/distribution threshold. You may not have known that we all cross over this threshold, but we do. There are two stages of our investment lives: accumulation and distribution. Your ability to understand these two stages can make or break both your pre-retirement and your retirement.

I don't know why, but when I think about the accumulation stage, I think about a squirrel hurrying to get as many nuts in the tree as possible before winter arrives. At first, the squirrel is calm and measured. He may even be complacent. "I've got plenty of time to prepare for the cold," he might think inside his squirrel brain. Of course, he's probably thinking this as he consumes the food that might serve him down the road. Hey, squirrels aren't necessarily immune to procrastination just because they're squirrels.

As winter nears, a sense of urgency joins the party. The squirrel realizes that he has only so much time before the nut-gathering season is over. If his food-store is light, he has to decide whether to take more risks to get the nuts he needs. Is he going to scurry out onto that high branch that doesn't exactly seem safe? Or is he going to adopt a new attitude of resourcefulness to bridge the gap between supply and demand?

All right, enough with the nutty metaphor. We only have so much time to accumulate financial resources. When that time ends, distribution begins. While this seems like a natural transition, it really isn't. The behavior, skills, and even risk tolerance you used to accumulate your assets all of a sudden need to change when you start to distribute your assets.

RISK

Every person decides how much risk he or she is willing to deal with. What most people don't realize is that you can't actually avoid risk. When people attempt to mitigate risk, they often expose themselves to different types of risk. This is especially true when it comes to financial planning.

Before we discuss some of the lesser-known financial risks, let's examine how you arrive at your personal risk tolerance. Simply put, risk tolerance is a measure of how much risk you are willing to accept in order to pursue investment returns. A low risk tolerance generally means you aren't willing to have your savings or investments decrease in value due to market activity. On the other hand, with a high risk tolerance, you are willing to accept fluctuations in account values, even when account values dip into the negative. The biggest drivers of risk tolerance are personal experience and philosophy, knowledge level, and time horizon.

Nothing destroys a moderate risk tolerance quite like an investment portfolio getting hammered. Even if the investments were suitable, reasonable, and appropriate, investment loss can significantly affect a person's willingness to take future risk, if and when the portfolio rises again. A negative experience can make people more introspective and conservative with their money.

I believe the number-one factor in determining risk tolerance is knowledge. People fear things they don't understand, as they should. If you don't understand investments and the financial markets, then frankly, you shouldn't proceed with investing anyway. The better solution would be to hire a trusted financial advisor and pair that person with a purposeful strategy to learn more about how the market works. If you don't know what you're doing with regard to investing, you refuse to hire an advisor, and you refuse to increase your financial education level, then you should have a low risk tolerance. It's self-preservation. It's necessary.

The final factor in determining risk tolerance is time horizon. Risk tolerance and time horizon have a very important relationship. As you get closer to the need for saved money, your time horizon shrinks, and your risk tolerance will almost always decrease. For example, when you're 30 years out from retirement, you may have a higher risk tolerance than you would when you're 30 days out from retirement.

Some people struggle to make wise retirement-planning decisions because they don't account for time horizon. Instead, they make their investment decisions solely based on their long-developed risk tolerance. In my opinion, this is a mistake. My theory on risk is simple: Never take an ounce of market risk more than you need to in order to accomplish your goal. Both risk tolerance and time horizon are factors in making this decision.

And then there are the numbers. As you saw in Chapter 6, taking market risk makes a significant impact on retirement. Based on 5,000 simulations of a retirement scenario using historical market returns, a person with a portfolio of 50 percent bond, 30 percent cash, and 20 percent stock has an 89 percent chance of having money left over after taking annual withdrawals of 4 percent (of total portfolio value) for 30 years. A person who has a 100 percent cash portfolio (money market and savings) has a 19 percent chance of having any money left over using the same withdrawal schedule. This makes the case that conservative investors often hurt themselves with conservative portfolio construction.

You should never invest against your risk tolerance. If you are a conservative investor, you are a conservative investor. There is no shame in that game. You shouldn't let anyone talk you out of being a conservative investor. The statistics I just mentioned shouldn't even talk you out of being a conservative investor. Feel free to educate yourself on the markets and investing, but if that doesn't make you feel less conservative, then don't change unless you're willing to accept the risk.

INFLATION

You know all that money you saved? It's getting less valuable every day. I know; that's a really sad thought. Inflation is a concept and real-world event that causes our money to lose purchasing power. Simply put, a loaf of bread cost you less last year than it does this year.

The Consumer Price Index (CPI) is the tool most often used when discussing and measuring inflation. The CPI examines a weighted average of prices of a basket of consumer goods and services, such as transportation, food, and medical care. As you know, when you're retired, your retirement income is primarily used to purchase things such as transportation, food, and medical care. See why your understanding of inflation is so important?

Over time, the cost of goods and services can increase. This is called *inflation*. If the cost of goods and services decreased, then we would be in a deflationary environment. While we could spend several pages discussing federal policy and the effects inflation and/or deflation have on our macroeconomy, let's not. Let's just focus our time on how inflation can impact your retirement.

For example, if $100 is able to buy your weekly groceries today, you need to understand how inflation affects the cost of those same groceries over time—and more importantly, how that affects your retirement cash flow. Specifically, based on historical CPI numbers, $100 of groceries in 1985 cost $202.65 in 2010. In just 25 years, the cost of goods doubled. If you are on a fixed income, like many retirees are, then inflation can create major issues for you late in retirement.

The solution is to make sure at least some of your retirement investments outpace inflation. Not only do you want your investments to grow so that you'll have more money than you started with, but you also want your investments to grow so that your initial investment principal doesn't suffer at the hands of inflating prices and decreasing purchasing power.

THE MAGICAL AGE

You are extremely close to a magical age. Once you surpass age 59-1/2, your retirement income options increase substantially. If you didn't know, 59-1/2 is the arbitrary age that was selected to determine when people would have access to their qualified investments (a.k.a. retirement accounts). When you pass that magical age, all the money you've saved for retirement becomes accessible instantly. Don't smile. Well, don't frown, either. Gaining access to your entire life savings on the day you hit 59-1/2 is undoubtedly exciting. But it really shouldn't matter to you.

You want to talk about messing up your retirement? Let's talk about when people gain access to their qualified retirement accounts and then start distributing money to themselves in order to do all sorts of random things. Of course it's your money, and you can do whatever you want with it, but you must keep things in perspective. That money is supposed to last you for the rest of your life.

TYPES OF INVESTMENTS AND INVESTMENT VEHICLES

Just because you may have stocks, bonds, and/or mutual funds, that doesn't necessarily mean you understand them the way you need to. As remedial as it may seem, take a moment to familiarize yourself with the important qualities of some very common investments often held by people in their sixties.

CERTIFICATE OF DEPOSIT (CD)

A Certificate of Deposit is a type of savings vehicle that is issued by a bank. It is an investment that is held for a fixed period of time and pays a fixed rate of interest. A CD is typically considered to be the most conservative investment vehicle out there. Unlike many other types of investments, CDs are insured by the FDIC.

Most CDs are issued and then held for somewhere between 30 days and 5 years. Due to their relatively low interest rates, CDs can struggle to keep pace with inflation. Although CDs can help you preserve your retirement money, they do very little to grow your retirement money or even preserve buying power. With inflation comes a loss of buying power.

STOCK

A stock is a share of the value of a company that can be purchased, sold, or traded as an investment. Although there are two main types of stocks—preferred stock and common stock—you're likely to be exposed only to common stock.

As an owner of preferred stock, you'll be among the first to receive dividends when the company either distributes extra cash during good times or liquidates assets during times of trouble. In addition, your dividend payout will be more consistent and predictable, as preferred stockholders are paid at regular intervals. The same does not apply to common stockholders. As an owner of common stock, you'll receive payouts only when the company's board of directors approves a payout. You'll also be the last to receive dividends during liquidation, as companies must pay all preferred stockholders before they pay common stockholders.

Some stocks pay you, as a partial owner of the company, a portion of the profits. This disbursement is called a *dividend*. The dividend may be 30 to 40 cents per share, or it may be up to $3 or $4. You can reinvest these dividends into more shares of stock through things like Dividend Reinvestment Programs (DRIPs).

All in all, when you own stock in a company, you own a piece of the company—albeit a small piece. It's not uncommon for retirees to utilize stock dividends as a way to create retirement income.

Your employer may even offer you stock, thus offering you partial ownership in the company you work for. If the amount of stock you end up accumulating is disproportionate to the rest of your investments, you may want to consider diversifying your investments (in other words, sell some of your company stock). You don't want your employment and your entire portfolio dependent on the same lever.

BOND

A bond is an investment in which you serve as the lender—to a company, to a bank, or to the government. They borrow your money and promise to pay you back in full, with interest payments.

The more respectable the institution—such as the U.S. government or a large-scale corporation with a track record of long-term success—the safer the investment. With safer investments come lower interest rates and lower payouts. The riskier the loan, the more interest is up for grabs. You've probably heard the term *junk bond*. It refers to a bond that isn't rated very highly, yet pays a pretty handsome amount of interest. The risk for default (the bond being worth nothing) is higher, but the returns can be great, too. This fact alone can dispel the myth that bonds are collectively safe.

In addition, the duration of the bond plays into how lucrative it might be for you—the longer the duration of the bond period, the higher the payout.

In the end, when you buy a bond, you let an institution borrow your money. Bonds are very common tools for retirees due to the guaranteed nature of bond interest. Additionally, municipal bonds are popular among retirees because of the tax-free income they provide.

MUTUAL FUND

A mutual fund is a collection of stocks and bonds managed by professional investors who diversify investments across a wide range of industries in an attempt to minimize risk. A mutual fund might contain investments in technology, agriculture, and pharmaceutical companies or any other industry, all in an attempt to ensure that the gains in one industry offset the losses in another.

Mutual funds earn income for you through the dividends on the stocks included in the fund and through interest from the bonds. If your stocks or bonds increase in price over the course of the year and your fund manager sells them at a higher price, the fund will experience a capital gain, the profits of which will be shared with investors.

EXCHANGE TRADED FUND

I should probably start by defining *index*. An index is a selection of stocks that is used to gauge the health and performance of the overall stock market. Whenever you hear or read "the market was up 38 points today," what they are talking about is the index. For instance, the Standard & Poor's 500 (S&P 500) Index is a group of 500 stocks that is used to measure the tone and direction of the stock market in general.

Exchange Traded Funds (ETFs) track the yields and returns of a specific index, such as the S&P 500 or the Dow Jones. Unlike other index funds, which try to beat the average performance of their index, an ETF attempts to mirror its index performance. In other words, if your Dow Jones ETF is performing exactly like the Dow Jones, it's doing well.

ETFs offer many of the same benefits of mutual funds—they're professionally managed and created to minimize risk—but the similarities end there. ETFs can be traded like a stock continually throughout the trading day, whereas mutual funds are priced only after the market closes. And because ETFs don't attempt to beat the market, they're less maintenance for managers, resulting in lower management fees.

As a result of these advantages, ETFs have become increasingly popular over the course of the last decade.

INDEX FUND

Index funds are similar to ETFs in that their success is tied to how well they replicate their index performance. For example, an index fund tracking the Dow Jones Industrial Average would own all of the same stocks as the Dow Jones.

Because index funds require minimal maintenance, they are passively managed. As a result, they have lower expense ratios (0.2 percent to 0.5 percent on average) than actively managed funds (which usually fall somewhere between 1.3 percent and 2.5 percent).

Index funds have grown in popularity both because of lower expense ratios and because market watchers realized that the indexes were outperforming mutual funds over the long term.

TARGET-DATE FUND

Target-date funds are investments that link investment selections with length of time from retirement. Each target-date fund is linked to a particular year—theoretically the year you wish to retire. Once you invest in this target-date fund, your investment allocation flows along what is called a *glide path*. This glide path consistently shifts the percentages of stock, bonds, and cash over time until they are at the "ideal" percentages to ready you for retirement. To add some additional complexity, a few target-date funds are meant to usher you through retirement, not just to retirement. The remainder of the target-date funds simply prepare your portfolio for retirement but aren't necessarily appropriate to hold when you are retired.

I've always thought of our investment allocations as cake recipes. Add the right amount of stock, the right amount of bonds, and the right amount of cash, and you will have a money-cake cooked to your liking. Target-date funds are prepackaged cakes. The ingredients are all right there, the cake is baked, and you can't adjust the recipe. Strangely, people mess up this part. If you have a target-date fund in your portfolio along with other funds, then you are basically pouring flour and/or sugar on the top of a prebaked cake that you just emptied into a mixing bowl from a plastic wrapper. Yeah, that's not going to taste good. When you combine a target-date fund with other investments in your account, you may create untended consequences. Target-date funds were designed to be the only investment in your account.

If I were forced to rank investing strategies within a retirement plan, target-date funds would find themselves in third place. In first place, you'd find a relationship with an investment advisor who can help you make the right investment selections according to both your risk tolerance and your time horizon. Second place belongs to educating yourself and managing your investments in a suitable, unemotional way. Realistically, educating yourself and managing your investments in a suitable, unemotional way is intensely challenging. Sound investment strategy isn't built on guts and panache; it's built on discipline and patience. And while doing it yourself is the second-best option, it's the worst option if you don't know what you're doing.

Which brings us to third place. Target-date funds are perfect for individuals who don't have an investment advisor and don't take the time to thoroughly educate themselves on the principles of investing. Target-date funds generally have slightly higher fees than a la carte investments, but there's an obvious reason for that. They're alive! The investment allocations shift as you get closer to your target retirement date, and you don't have to do anything.

IRA

Once you achieve the age of 59-1/2, you have unfettered access to your Individual Retirement Account (IRA), also called a traditional IRA. You can put almost any type of investment inside of an IRA, including stocks, bonds, mutual funds, ETFs, and/or index funds. Depending on your income, contributions to an IRA may be deductible on your income tax filing. They essentially have the same tax status as a 401(k). Additionally, an IRA allows your investments to grow without being subjected to capital gains or dividend income taxes. However, when you receive IRA distributions during retirement, your distributions will be considered income and will be subject to income tax.

You will be required to distribute money out of your IRA no later than age 70-1/2. This is called a *Required Minimum Distribution* (RMD). As you know, money within an IRA has never been taxed. Uncle Sam wants his cut, and thus you are required to take a distribution in order to create a taxable event. You must make your first withdrawal no later than April 1st following the year in which you reach age 70-1/2. You will then need to take distributions from your IRA every year for the rest of your life. Again, Uncle Sam needs the tax revenue. It's not personal; it's just business. Well, not really business. It's just taxes.

Your RMD is calculated by dividing the prior year-end fair market value of the retirement account by the applicable distribution period or life expectancy. The company that holds your IRA will calculate your RMD for you.

ROTH IRA

A Roth IRA is fully accessible when you reach 59-1/2 years old. If you have a Roth IRA, it was funded with after-tax money, which means you will not have to pay any additional taxes upon taking withdrawals from your Roth. Since your Roth IRA will continue to grow tax-deferred indefinitely, many retirees choose to put their Roth IRA distributions off as long as they can. There are absolutely no RMDs for Roth IRAs. That's a good thing!

401(k)

Most employers offer 401(k) plans as part of their compensation packages. A 401(k) enables you to make a contribution of each paycheck into a tax-deferred plan. Many employers offer a matching program, in which they will match your contribution up to a specified limit. So if the 401(k) match limit is 3 percent and you contribute 3 percent of your salary, your employer will match it, creating a total investment of 6 percent of your salary into your plan.

Needless to say, you should always save at least the maximum amount of your employer match, or you'll be leaving money on the table. And that's never a good thing. But since you're in your fifties, you really should make it a goal to max out your company-sponsored retirement plan. Yes, I realize that's more than $20,000 per year, but it's reasonable to suggest that your income in retirement might dip by $20,000 or so, so why not get used to living without the extra money? Besides, maxing out your retirement plan makes sense tax-wise, helps you accumulate retirement assets, and breaks your dependency on your work income.

529 COLLEGE SAVINGS PLAN

Qualified tuition programs—or 529s, as most people call them—were created under the Small Business Job Protection Act of 1996. They work a lot like Roth IRAs in terms of taxation, but 529 plans are designed to help you save for a college education. It can be your college education, your child's college education, or even your grandchild's education. It doesn't really matter.

Every state has its own 529 College Savings Plan. You can invest your money in any of them. You don't have to go to school or live in the state of the plan in which you invest, either. Many people, myself included, choose the 529 plan in the state in which they live because of the state tax benefits. However, every state has different ways in which it incentivizes or doesn't incentivize depositors to save for college. Although fees and investment performance are certainly important factors in making your 529 selection, state tax benefits are hard to pass up. If your state has allowed for tax credits or anything else of the sort in relation to depositing into a 529 College Savings Plan, you should explore it thoroughly before looking to another state's plan.

ANNUITY

When you invest in an annuity, you give your money to a life insurance company that attempts to grow it. The life insurance company helps mitigate the risks associated with investing, whether by guaranteeing returns or by guaranteeing fixed payments to you at a later date for a set period of time.

Many people utilize annuities to ensure a steady stream of income during retirement. There are two primary ways in which an annuity can provide retirement income: annuitization or withdrawals. When you annuitize an annuity, you give up rights to the principal in order to receive fixed lifetime monthly payments. While giving up access to a giant chuck of money doesn't exactly sound fun, it can actually make sense in certain instances.

Annuities have the reputation for being expensive. It is true that annuities can be much more expensive than mutual funds and ETFs, but the reason for the added expense is that there are typically guarantees associated with annuities. Because life insurance is involved, the additional expense purchases risk mitigation from the insurance company. You just need to decide how much you are willing to pay to receive a set of guarantees.

If you choose to go the annuity route, make sure you understand exactly what the fees are buying you. There are three primary types of annuities, and each one comes with its own unique set of fees. The first type of annuity—a fixed annuity—is pretty straightforward. Your fees will be primarily limited to mortality and expense charges, or M&E, as industry people call them. They are called *fixed* annuities because you will typically receive a fixed rate on your investment principal.

Index annuities are the second primary type. These annuities are linked to market indexes and are meant to allow you to participate in the upside of the market and protect you from market downswings. In doing so, your gains typically capped. For instance, your cap may be 8 percent. This means if the market (usually the S&P 500) increases in value by 20 percent in a particular year, then your gains would be limited to just 8 percent. However, if the market were to fall 20 percent, you generally wouldn't take any loss at all. Your annuity wouldn't be credited with any gains during the down years, but you also wouldn't lose a penny. The capped nature of index annuities can make them seem expensive. If the market does 20 percent and you get 8 percent, one might argue that you paid a 12 percent fee.

A variable annuity is far and away the most complicated type. It can involve both significant risk and significant expense. That doesn't make it bad, but you should fully take the time to understand *all* of the moving pieces of a variable annuity before you purchase one. The expenses for a variable annuity can approach 4 percent annually, once you figure in the expenses for each individual investment within the plan.

It's very common to purchase riders on all types of annuities, especially variable annuities. A rider is a bell and whistle, if you will. It enhances the annuity by guaranteeing various elements of the plan. For example, a rider may guarantee that your variable annuity grows at no less than 5 percent per year, or it may guarantee that you can take extra income off of the annuity if you are in a long-term care facility.

From what I've seen, the fifties is the primary decade in which people enter into annuity contracts. Annuities aren't bad investments, per se. They are just complicated, more permanent in nature than most people are used to, and often over-prescribed.

HIRING A FINANCIAL ADVISOR

Financial advisors are like wine. A higher price point doesn't always equal better results. On top of that, as with wine, personal preference and tastes can dictate the consumer's experience and satisfaction. Every person in the world besides you may like a particular wine, but if you don't like it, what's the point of drinking it? You need to understand how your priorities, attitude, and personality intersect with a potential advisor's offerings.

How do you select the right financial advisor? It's a very simple question that elicits stress, fear, and confusion in the average financial consumer. And it's a question that I never fully understood until I stopped working with personal financial planning clients. From the outset, the process of selection is overwhelming. Consider the titles alone. How would you even begin to decipher the following jargon?

Financial planner. Investment planner. Investment advisor. Financial consultant. Financial advisor. Registered representative. Financial specialist. Agent. Retirement planner. College planner. Broker.

In the words of my precocious four-year-old, "Good luck with that."

And if you make the right title choice, you'll next need to decide what you want out of an advisor relationship. If you choose to hire a financial advisor, you should expect the person to serve two primary functions. First, your advisor should help you find and evaluate investment opportunities. Second, your advisor should move you forward financially. Your net worth should increase. This means that your debts should decrease and your savings and investments should increase. While these are the reasons to hire a good financial advisor, you'll still need to make sense of who to hire.

You really only need a financial advisor if you are going to invest. It has been my experience that financial advisors offer very little expertise in anything other than investing and technical financial planning. By the way, debt and budgeting generally fall outside this expertise. A good financial advisor will be important to your future. Once you've cleaned up all your debt, budgeting issues, and discipline issues, like we all have to, then follow these tips to pick a great financial advisor.

▶ **Knowledge.** It's even weird to write about this. A great majority of financial-industry people have no idea what they're doing. In fact, in 2012 a cat named Orlando outperformed a number of investment advisors in the U.K. And no, I don't mean cat as in he was a cool cat.

I mean he had whiskers and drank out of a saucer. Orlando threw his toy on a grid filled with different options. Where his toy landed is where the money was invested. The cat dominated the experts who were using "traditional" means. And by traditional means I mean no batting a cat toy across a grid of investments.

No one knows what the market is going to do. No one. They might have a theory as to why it might go up or down, but they don't actually know. Financial advisors love to compare themselves to doctors, but I hope that doctors don't guess as much as financial advisors do. This isn't meant to be overcritical; it's just fact. You simply want your financial advisor to position you in the best possible manner so that you can do well in good markets and survive in bad markets. Anyone else that tells you they can do something different from this is lying. Come to think of it, this first quality should probably be "humility paired with knowledge." Your financial advisor should be able to give you confidence via his or her vulnerability. Several financial advisors try to gain your confidence by appearing all-knowing. That's a bad idea, especially if a cat named Orlando just beat their returns.

▶ **Attentiveness.** No one likes to be ignored. I've accidentally neglected to return phone calls. I've accidentally neglected to return emails. Does this mean I'm terrible at customer service? To some, it may seem that way. The reality is that no matter the industry, customer service is really important, yet at times people make mistakes. When money is involved—all the money you have ever saved—things can get extra stressful when a phone call isn't returned. You'll know if your advisor is ducking you. You should meet with your advisor at least once per year, and the responsibility for setting up this meeting is shared.

▶ **Ability to teach.** Do you know what an American Depositary Receipt (ADR) is? No? That's okay; you wouldn't be in the minority. If you work with a good advisor for long enough, you will learn stuff like this and be better for it. I tend to eat at restaurants that make me a better home cook. Somehow, some way, I learn things about cooking by interacting with the waitstaff or kitchen staff. Have you been with a financial advisor for five years, yet you haven't learned anything? That's bad. Make sure you are a better investor for having known the advisor you're working with.

▶ **Risk radar.** Do you want to hear something crazy but true? I became a riskier investor, personally, when I stopped investing other people's money. Weird, right? I don't think so. My theory is that I never wanted my personal risk tolerance, derived from years of study and experience, to bleed over into my clients' risk tolerance. It'd be like trying to convince someone to like spicy food, despite the fact that it gives them ulcers. If you don't want to take risks with your money, then don't. My least favorite thing about the investment industry is that if your advisor is wrong, then you are the one who suffers. You should dictate the direction of your investments by allowing the advisor to thoroughly measure your risk tolerance.

▶ **Reasonable fees.** Did you notice that I didn't say *fee only* or *commission only*? Why? Because, frankly, I've learned that it doesn't matter. The theory in the fee-based financial planning community (advisors that charge either a flat rate or a percentage of your assets invested) is that the only way to ensure objective advice is to limit compensation to the fee-based method. This is a fallacy. A commission salesperson isn't inherently biased. Would you rather have a commission-based financial advisor who knows what he or she is doing or a fee-based advisor who simply passed a test? Compensation structure is not a tell. You can't smoke out a crook by looking only at how someone is compensated. Some of the top Ponzi schemes of all time were perpetrated by fee-based advisors (Bernie Madoff). Just make sure your advisor has reasonable fees. And we'll leave it at that.

Here's the crazy thing about these five qualities: Everyone will measure them differently, just like wine. Some of my past clients may have thought I struggled at any one, if not all, of the qualities listed above. And because it's their perspective and their perspective alone, they'd be right. This is why advisor ratings—and wine ratings, for that matter—should be taken with a grain of salt. I've always thought advisor ratings were silly. I was once ranked as a top advisor at one of the firms I worked for. The rankings were based on production and nothing else. I was rated as excellent because I produced a lot of revenue for the firm, not because I was objectively good. Oddly enough, I've seen several advisors at the top of several companies leave the industry due to ethical and disciplinary issues. On top of that, many advisor ratings are linked to advertising buys.

This is why you should interview potential advisors and not just blindly go with the person a friend recommends. I love my friends, but I hate some of their wine recommendations. Do your best to try to evaluate these five qualities during your interview. My bottom line is this: You should be treated how you want to be treated by someone who knows what they're doing, all the while understanding your risk tolerance and charging you moderate fees.

But maybe the bigger point is this: You need to clean up your habits before you bother with an investment advisor, anyway.

FEES FOR A FINANCIAL ADVISOR

The financial planning industry has a practical, yet insincere solution to the advisor selection quandary. The people in the industry have decided to turn the question into one of compensation. This path makes some sense, yet it offers close to zero solutions for those people without investable assets. In other words, if you don't have copious amounts of money to invest, then you will be passed over by the industry ethicists, the fee-based advisors, and fee-only advisors. This is where the confusion really begins.

There are primarily three ways in which financial advisors are compensated: commission-based, fee-based, and fee-only.

A commission-based advisor doesn't charge fees, but instead is compensated by investment and insurance companies upon selling their investments to consumers. And as crazy as this sounds, commission-based advisors have no industry-regulated responsibility to do what's in the client's best interest. This is called *fiduciary responsibility*, and commission-based advisors don't have it. Is a commission-based advisor predestined to give you biased financial advice based on potential commission rates? Arguably, but not always. Some experts argue that human nature prevents commission-based advisors from giving objective financial advice. I disagree.

A fee-based advisor charges a fee to manage investment assets and can still accept commissions from insurance and investment companies, whereas a fee-only advisor collects a fee for managing your money but doesn't accept any commission from third parties. The idea is to create an objective environment of fiduciary responsibility. However, the assertion that a fee-based or fee-only advisor is undeniably scrupulous is absurd. You do realize that speed-limit signs aren't suggestions, right? The main problem with this method is the imposition of "minimum assets" policies.

For a moment, let's say you have $8,000 to your name. Is that a lot of money? If you only have $8,000, then it's a tremendous amount of money. In fact, it's 100 percent of your money. Do you want it invested wisely? Yes. Do you want it invested in an unbiased way? Yes. Do you want someone to pick up the phone when you call to find someone to invest your money? Yes. The only person likely to pick up the phone is going to be a commission-based advisor.

This is a problem that the industry has created. The industry has basically said, "If you have $50,000 to invest, then we've got several ways in which the industry can objectively serve you." That doesn't work for me. Fee-based and fee-only advisors typically have minimum client requirements. I don't begrudge businesspeople's right to make business decisions on who they want or don't want as clients, but the scrutiny being placed on commission-based advisors for taking on smaller clients is unjust. This is all to say that picking your advisor based on how they're compensated is popular and convenient, but overrated.

No matter what type of advisor you choose, you owe it to yourself and your money to do a broker check. A broker check will allow you to see the regulatory history of your advisor. You'll be able to see complaints, judgments, and interesting patterns. Should you then make your judgment solely on what you find on the advisor's broker check? Nope. But I wouldn't consider hiring an advisor without first running a broker check. You can run a check on your advisor at BrokerCheck.FINRA.org.

DEALING WITH REALITY

Now that you've addressed debt, learned to budget, learned about making major purchases, discussed credit, and learned about savings and investing, it's time to have a very uncomfortable talk. Sometimes life goes extra wrong, in spite of all your diligence and planning. For those moments, you can turn to one place: insurance.

CHAPTER 8

THE PITFALLS: INSURANCE

You have purchased several types of insurance in your lifetime. In fact you've probably bought a combination of life, disability, health, car, homeowners, and some other form of insurance. That's a lot of premiums. I'm pretty confident you have spent hundreds of thousands of dollars on insurance. Those different types of insurances have protected you and have provided relief in the event that you needed to file a claim.

Your insurance needs will continue to evolve throughout your life. As you progress through your fifties and into your sixties, your primary method of funding your healthcare needs will shift, and you need to become vigilant about protecting the assets you've accumulated. You may even start dropping different types of insurance.

For instance, you may consider dropping your disability insurance coverage or large amounts of term life insurance. But remember, dropping your life insurance and/or disability insurance is only prudent when you become somewhat self-insured. In other words, you have accumulated enough money that the impact of your death or disability becomes financially insignificant. And second, your insurance needs will not only shift you out of some products, but also shift you into some products.

At this point in your life, you should be primarily concerned with a few different types of insurance: health insurance, Medicare, long-term care insurance, and life insurance.

TYPES OF INSURANCE

Here's what you need to know about each type of insurance coverage at this point in your life. Additionally, you'll find a few pointers on how to make each of these coverages work even better for you and your financial goals.

CAR

Everybody wants car insurance protection, but nobody wants to deal with having car insurance. Like most other types of insurance, car insurance can be extremely frustrating because it only pays off when something bad happens. You pray that you never need it; thus, in a way, you're praying that you waste every dollar ever spent on car insurance coverage.

However, there are good financial decisions and bad financial decisions to be had when selecting car insurance coverage. What is the point having inadequate insurance coverage? Don't be shortsighted. You need to pay attention to this stuff. Some of it saves you money on your premiums. And some of these tips make your life easier if an accident ever were to happen. Following you will find what I find to be the five silliest car insurance mistakes.

▶ **Having too low of a deductible.** If you have an emergency fund that allow you to handle an insurance deductible regardless of whether it's $500 or $1,000, then set your deductible at $1,000. There's no reason to pay the additional premium necessary to secure a low deductible. As you may or may not know, a deductible is the portion of money you are responsible for if you were to file a claim. In other words, if you have a $500 deductible, then you are responsible for the first $500 of costs associated with making you whole. Why waste money on a lower premium when you've got the means to handle an emergency?

▶ **Having no rental car coverage.** If you do get into an accident and lose the use of your car, you may be in trouble. Many people lack free access to another vehicle. So for practicality's sake, having rental car reimbursement coverage on your auto policy can prevent your life from getting crazy-hectic while your car is getting repaired. You don't necessarily need this coverage if you have access to another vehicle or you can seamlessly carpool, but I find that most people should strongly consider rental car reimbursement coverage.

▶ **Having too low of liability limits.** Auto insurance helps you repair your car in the event of an accident. But auto insurance also protects your assets if you were to cause serious damage to someone else. If your liability limits are too low and you are subject to a judgment higher than your limits, then your personal assets can be seized. That's as awful as it sounds.

▶ **Not getting competitive quotes.** Every car insurance company has its own secret recipe of herbs and spices. This is to say that every auto insurance company calculates premiums differently. Some companies put more dependency on your age, gender, driving record, and/or credit score than other companies might. This means there is an auto insurance company that happens to match up with you and your characteristics, and your job is to figure out which company it is. If you choose to have the same insurance company for years on end, just know that you are likely paying way too much for car insurance. This isn't to say you should switch every year, but you should periodically check and see whether you can save money on comparable coverage.

▶ **Filing too many claims.** Look, I know this advice is not what you want to hear, but filing claims can be a really bad idea. Your insurance premium will go up if you file an insurance claim. In fact, if you file too many claims, your insurance company may drop you. I know, I know. What's the point of insurance if you can't use it? You need to think of your car insurance as catastrophic coverage. Don't file silly little claims that your deductible would absorb anyway. Be smart. This requires restraint, math, and a healthy dose of reality.

Car insurance is a necessary financial tool. Don't be in such a hurry that you neglect to make wise decisions with regard to your coverage choices. It also pays to have a great agent who can explain these concepts to you.

TEEN DRIVERS

If children are part of your world, then you must also understand car insurance as it relates to teen drivers. Teens have a reputation for being...um...bad drivers. Don't believe me? Look at the cost to insure them as drivers. Teens speed. Teens wreck. And teens don't make the best driving decisions. You know this for one reason: You were once a teen, too.

Be sure your liability limits on your auto insurance policy reflect the fact that you have a teen driver. In fact, you may want to consider getting additional liability protection through the purchase of an umbrella policy. An umbrella policy provides liability protection above and beyond both your auto and homeowners insurance liability limits. Your assets are at risk if your liability limits are too low. If you were sued and you didn't have enough liability protection, a judgment could result in a financial catastrophe.

RENTERS

Renting is increasingly more common in the United States. According to a study done by Harvard, the renting population in the U.S. grew from 31 percent in 2004 to 35 percent in 2012. Renting is no longer just for a transitional or temporary situation. This natural progression of renting as a more stable lifestyle should lead to insurance, but it has not. The Insurance Information Institute reported that as of 2014, only 37 percent of renters have insurance. This is a big problem. You protect yourself with health and life insurance; it's time you start protecting your stuff.

Your landlord's insurance doesn't cover you. This is the most common myth about renting: You assume your landlord's insurance will cover you. Well, it does cover the house or apartment you are renting, but it doesn't cover your stuff. If your apartment burns down, the apartment will get rebuilt with your landlord's insurance money, but all your stuff will be gone. This is the single most important reason why you need renters insurance.

Additionally, renters insurance is cheap. Unlike other types of insurance, renters insurance is actually extremely affordable. For less than $200 a year, you can insure all your stuff. That's an amazing deal. The thing about insurance—all insurance—is that you hope you don't have to use it. So you may argue it's just throwing away $200 a year, but chances are you throw away more than $200 regularly on junk that doesn't serve nearly as important a role as renters insurance. The small price tag is a more than justified expense.

HOMEOWNERS

You know the old saying: With great homeownership comes great responsibility—or something like that. I think I just lifted and then butchered that saying from a *Spiderman* movie. Your economic risks spike when you become a homeowner. Storms, floods, fires, and even your neighbor slipping and falling on your steps all become your problem when you become a homeowner.

Think of homeowners insurance like renters insurance, except homeowners insurance covers the structure too, as well as liability. While a landlord has to deal with insuring the building in which you live when you're a renter, you have to insure everything when you're a homeowner. You are even financially responsible for events that take place on your property.

If your dog bites someone, or your tree falls on your neighbor's house, or a worker is injured while repairing something in your house, you may be liable for damages. Your homeowners insurance will pay to defend you from any lawsuits and will cover any judgments up to your liability. So, you should take some time to determine the proper amount of liability limits to have on your homeowners insurance policy, based on factors such as your income and lifestyle. You'd be surprised how many insurance companies will refuse you coverage, based on strange factors such as what breed of dog you have.

In most instances, your homeowners insurance premium will be paid through your mortgage company. Your mortgage company usually collects monies, in addition to your principal and interest payments, to pay for your property taxes and homeowners insurance. These additional payments flow into something called an *escrow account*. When your property taxes or insurance invoice is due, the escrow account pays the bill. On a side note, you'll notice that your mortgage payment will increase when your property taxes or homeowners insurance premiums increase.

HEALTH

Fortunately for you, the trend in healthcare today points consumers to what is called *consumer-driven healthcare*. It's a concept that not only protects you, it also rewards you for low-risk behavior. It consists of a health savings account (HSA), paired with a high-deductible health insurance plan. I've come to the conclusion that an HSA is a great decision, especially for those who are not only healthy but also fiscally responsible. And given that you're reading a book about how to be financially responsible, it may be the perfect strategy for you.

The key is the HSA. Instead of putting all of your budgeted money toward a traditional health insurance plan that features co-pays, prescription drug coverage, and relatively low deductibles, an HSA paired with a high-deductible health insurance plan splits money into two pots. The first pot of money is used to pay for your health insurance coverage. The second pot of money is deposited into your HSA, where it sits until you have healthcare costs. Don't have any healthcare costs? Then keep the money in your HSA. The money that is in your HSA will always be yours, and it has no expiration date in terms of use. You can use the money in your HSA to fund medical expenses throughout the rest of your life, including the costs associated with Medicare. And once you reach the age of 65, you can use the money in your HSA for nonmedical expenses, but you will have to pay income tax on the money you distribute for those nonmedical expenditures. In traditional health insurance, you may have co-pays for doctor's office visits and prescriptions, none of which typically go toward your overall deductible. However, when using an HSA paired with a high-deductible health insurance plan, you pay for all medical expenses until you reach your deductible.

You pay for prescriptions, procedures, and non-wellness office visits with money from your HSA. Wellness visits generally cost you nothing, and several employers have begun to aggressively make additional HSA contributions on your behalf. This can create some short-term cash-flow crunches, but an HSA makes a ton of long-term sense.

HSAs also offer brilliant tax features. The money in an HSA is said to be "triple tax advantaged." This is to suggest that deposits into the account occur pre-tax, the growth in the account is tax-deferred, and the withdrawals for medical purposes are tax-free. Technically, that's better than a 401(k).

When you start an HSA, things can be hairy for the first couple of months, until your HSA balance starts to climb. I recently ran across a company that deposited about $1,300 into employee HSAs after the employees completed certain wellness activities, thus making good health a financial incentive for employees.

Ultimately, though, this is all about being proactive. In your financial life, proactive is budgeting, building an emergency fund, and staying out of debt. That way, when life happens, you are prepared. Does losing your job stink? Absolutely. But having three months' worth of income set aside in your emergency fund helps smooth out the bumps.

As healthcare consumers, we've been trained to be reactive. We pay a bunch of nonrefundable money (premiums), and then we care about our health when something goes wrong. This is incredibly backwards. HSAs switch up this backward dynamic.

If you're given the option, an HSA paired with a high-deductible health insurance plan should be your choice.

LIFE

When you're in your fifties, life insurance can serve several different purposes, from the practical to the ingenious.

But what if you currently don't have dependents? Why do you need life insurance then? Let's examine all the reasons why someone would purchase life insurance regardless of whether they have dependents, and we'll see whether the answer exists within these reasons.

▶ **To cover survivor needs.** When you die, your income dies. Your dependents' needs will persist long after you are gone. No dependents generally equals no survivor needs.

▶ **To cover final expenses.** Your family is already upset that you're dead; don't stick them with the funeral bill. A funeral costs between $5,000 and $20,000. You don't really want to force your nondependent family members to pick up that tab in their time of grief.

▶ **To pay off your debts.** If you are the only signer for your debt, then your debts will be paid by your assets upon your death. If you don't have enough assets to offset your debt, then the lender is up a creek. However, if you have a cosigner, then your cosigner is fully responsible for your debt at the time of your death. Yikes. If you owe money to anyone or you have had anyone cosign on a loan, then please buy enough life insurance to cover your debt.

▶ **For estate planning purposes.** Life insurance is often purchased to provide a means of paying estate taxes upon the insured's death. That way, beneficiaries aren't faced with an eroding inheritance, which can often be devastated by estate taxes. Talk to your attorney about using life insurance to protect your money if creating generational wealth is important to you.

TYPES OF LIFE INSURANCE

There are two primary types of life insurance that you need to understand. And unless you have a financial obligation that is temporary in nature, only one of the types of life insurance is appropriate for someone in his or her fifties.

Term life insurance, as opposed to permanent life insurance, which is sometimes called *whole-life* or *universal life*, is temporary coverage. You buy term life insurance usually in blocks of time. For instance, you could buy a $250,000 20-year term policy. The policy would pay your beneficiaries the face amount ($250,000) in the event of your death, as long as your death occurred within the 20-year coverage period.

Permanent coverage provides—you guessed it!—permanent coverage as long as you continue to make premium payments. Most permanent life insurance policies build up a cash component within the policy. It is called *cash value*. Cash value can be borrowed against or withdrawn from the life insurance policy. In some instances, the cash value builds up enough value that you are able to stop making premium payments, and the policy ends up paying for itself. Permanent insurance, by its nature, is much more expensive than term life insurance, but then again it offers several more features.

If you were 30 years old, I don't think it would particularly matter what type of life insurance you had, as long as you bought the right amount of coverage. If you needed $250,000 of life insurance and all you could afford was term coverage, then you should buy the term coverage. If you needed $250,000 of life insurance and all you could afford of the permanent coverage was $50,000, then you should buy the term coverage.

You may not even need life insurance at all. If you have enough money for your survivors, you have no debts, and your health insurance plan is adequate to cover catastrophic illnesses, which often bring bills after death, then direct your insurance dollars elsewhere.

The most important aspect of life insurance is getting enough coverage for the period you are trying to cover. Your goal should be to become self-insured. That means you don't need life insurance because you have enough permanent income streams and assets to provide for your survivors in the event of your death.

If you're single, you don't have debt, you have enough cash money to cover your funeral expenses, and you have resolved not to have any financial dependents, then you don't need life insurance. Don't buy it.

One strategy you can employ is to take advantage of your life insurance benefits through your employer. I generally prefer that people have life insurance outside of their group coverage because of portability issues (the inability to take the coverage with you to your next job). However, in this instance group coverage is a decent temporary fix to your problem, if you are unsure of what to do.

Make It Easy on Your Survivors

When you die, your passwords die, too. When you die, the peculiar place where you keep your business documents remains peculiar—and unfound. And when you die, the financial role you have held in your family is relinquished immediately.

I'm reminded of a financial disaster I cleaned up just a few years ago. Money wasn't the issue, yet it was a financial emergency nonetheless. There was plenty of money and life insurance, but there were absolutely no transition plans. How does a surviving spouse re-create the daily financial doings of a person who dies?

A widow came to me shortly after her husband passed away for help organizing her financial life. She started the meeting by saying, "He had two different businesses with two different checkbooks, and he had two different credit cards at two different companies. Every phone call I make in order to make progress creates three new phone calls. He was such a private person that he never wanted me to worry about money. Although he left me plenty of money, I have to unwind his businesses, and I'm so scared."

Money isn't everything. Death begets loss. Loss begets grief. Grief and disorganization beget anger. It's quite common for people to say things such as, "The most loving thing you can do for your surviving spouse is to make sure that you leave them adequate life insurance." This is true, but leaving money for someone isn't enough.

The Internet has changed the game when it comes to survivor transitions, and not in a good way. All generations are at risk. Baby boomers were socialized with traditional gender roles. This means that men primarily dealt with the family finances. The death of a male baby boomer sends shockwaves through his family. While the death of a female baby boomer is equally awful, the financial transition isn't as severe based on how 1950s gender roles were established. This is a real problem.

Here are the things you need to consider to help make the worst moment in your loved one's life a little easier.

1. **Have a password plan.** I use a password vault program, such as LastPass. I have one password to remember, and the rest of the passwords are managed by the vault. My wife needs to know just one password, and she can open the vault to all my other passwords. It's secure, and it's the best way for your loved one to access your important information.

2. **Discuss your job.** Your significant other needs to know important details about your business/job. He or she needs to know where you bank, where your retirement accounts are, and many other details. Your spouse also needs to be aware of your business advisors, your lawyer, your accountant, and any financial advisors.

3. **Lift the curtain.** Do you have weird financial habits? Yeah, me too. Please, please, *please* let your partner know what's going on. Regular budget meetings can help, and regular discussions about your financial life can make all the difference in the world.

4. **Ask up.** Ask your parents what their plan is. Don't get this twisted, though: You aren't asking about their finances, you're asking about their transition plan. It's a

loving conversation. "Dad, where do you bank? Who's your lawyer? What do I need to know to take care of mom when you die?"

5. **Ask down.** Ask your adult children what their plans are. It's show and tell—you show them your plan and then ask to see their plan. Discuss the importance of a healthy transition plan.

Your significant others' right to grieve peacefully is important. Allow them to do this. Once again, to be clear, this has nothing to do with money. It's all about organization.

LONG-TERM CARE

Long-term care insurance is not a product that enjoys the public's full comprehension. I believe this willful ignorance is based on denial. People don't want to picture themselves in an eldercare scenario. Ask 100 people what they know about long-term care insurance, and 95 people will prove that their knowledge is limited to "it's nursing-home insurance." Sure, long-term care insurance can help pay for a stay in a nursing home. But it's so much more.

Your stay in a long-term care facility will get paid for one way or another. I'm not expressing an overly optimistic perspective here. If you need to get eldercare, you'll get it. The question is who will pay for it and what the indirect costs will be. Activities of Daily Living (ADLs) are the standard litmus test for required care. For instance, if you can't bathe, feed, dress, or transport yourself, then you are likely to need organized assistance. A long-term care insurance policy will help pay for your care when you can't perform two or more ADLs (depending on the policy). However, if you don't have a long-term care insurance policy, you will need to pay for your own care. Paying for your own care is where things start to spin out of control.

First, nursing care, in-home care, or adult day services are not cheap. It's not unusual for a one-year stay in a long-term care facility to cost you $60,000. A three-year stay, with constantly increasing costs, will cost you around $200,000. Long-term care insurance mitigates these costs and in turn protects your assets. And while protecting your assets might not seem like a priority compared to your health, it is essential if you have a significant other who currently doesn't need eldercare. Long-term care insurance pays for your stay and protects your assets so that your partner doesn't run out of money. If you need your assets to fund your stay, then what is the person you've left at home supposed to do? How will your loved one be able to financially survive when your joint assets are being used to pay for terribly expensive care?

The answers to these seemingly impossible questions vary in negativity, but none of them is positive. Children and grand-children often step in and assist in whatever way they can. But the additional expenses shouldered by your family members push back their retirement planning, their college planning, and even their ability to make their own long-term care prepa-rations. Admittedly, the idea of family stepping in to help seems natural and somewhat expected, but that doesn't mean it's not without damaging financial ramifications. Long-term care insurance helps keep people from unleashing avoidable financial shrapnel on their families.

When your assets have been spent to pay for your long-term care stay, or if you didn't have any assets to begin with, you will transition into Medicaid eligibility. Medicaid has very stringent income and asset requirements. Don't read this as "you have to achieve a certain amount of money"; read this as "you don't get to keep much money" to be eligible for Medicaid. Once you've drained a vast majority of your household assets, your long-term care stay will be covered by Medicaid, and your significant other will be left in the family home with very few resources.

Like most health-related insurance, long-term care insurance is least expensive when you are young and healthy. Most couples should start looking at long-term care insurance options when they hit their early fifties. Your fifties are your prime earning years, and you should be able to adjust your budget to handle the monthly premiums. Waiting until your sixties will make the coverage more expensive but no less important.

Increased longevity has brought us many positive considerations, but unfortunately, extended long-term care stays, which are a side effect of increased longevity, are now more common than ever. Long-term care insurance is a relatively new tool that helps families address the financial effects of eldercare needs. Explore long-term care insurance for your own good, as well as that of your significant other and your family. Proper planning can help you avoid very avoidable problems.

CONSIDER GETTING AN INSURANCE AGENT

Buying insurance over the phone or the Internet is as popular as ever, but that doesn't mean it's the right thing to do. Can you save a few bucks by buying coverage through a call center? Sure. Can that same call center be there when you have questions? Sure. But you are paying a ton of money for insurance across the board. You deserve to fully understand your coverage, and you deserve to have an advocate. I don't want to talk to a different person every time I have an insurance question. I want a reliable and constant source of information and assistance. A personal relationship with an insurance agent is a great relationship to have; the services an insurance agent provides can be an amazing tool to have when emergencies arrive.

PREPARING FOR INSURANCE IN YOUR SIXTIES

The insurance that you need and have in your fifties isn't terribly different from the insurance you've had your entire life, with the exception of long-term care insurance. But when you hit your sixties, a lot will change. The major changes are in relation to your health insurance coverage, primarily the introduction of Medicare into your life.

Whereas you can't exactly do anything in your fifties that would impact your Medicare choices in your sixties, it is important you understand the ins and outs of Medicare so you can budget for it.

MEDICARE

In the United States, once you reach the age of 65, your primary healthcare plan is Medicare. Medicare was created in 1965 by the Johnson Administration as a way to guarantee insurability for those over the age of 65. And although Medicare is a welcome relief for many people as they reach age 65, there are still a number of confusing elements that leave retirees with less coverage than they had originally counted on, as well as more expenses.

To begin, Medicare isn't free. It's obviously not free to administer, and it isn't free for the covered person. This is where the confusion can begin. There are four parts to Medicare. They are aptly named Part A, Part B, Part C, and Part D. Some of the parts are free for most people, some of the parts are optional, and some of the parts can cost you a significant amount of money every month.

In most circumstances, you must sign up for Medicare within a seven-month window surrounding the age at which you become Medicare eligible. This typically means you must sign up for coverage sometime between three months prior to when you turn 65 and four months after you turn 65. If you don't sign up within this window, you may face a penalty if you aren't part of an exception to the rule.

You won't get notice that you need to sign up unless you are already receiving Social Security. If you're like most people, 65 has always stuck out in your mind as an important age. Leverage this feeling to make sure you sign up for Medicare on time. You don't want to get tied up in the penalties and delays.

PART A

When you sign up for Medicare, you automatically are enrolled in Part A, while all the other parts are optional.

A vast majority of people don't pay for Medicare Part A. Okay, that isn't exactly true. A vast majority of people have already paid for Medicare Part A. You know that pesky deduction from your paycheck that said "Medicare" on the line item? That was you paying for Medicare Part A. If you aren't eligible for premium-free Part A, then you will have to pay for it. It can cost you in excess of $400 per month.

Part A primarily covers hospital stays and skilled nursing care stays. Of course, there's more to it than that. You will pay nothing for the first 60 days of a hospitalization, and then you are subjected to a deductible in excess of $1,200 per benefit period.

As mentioned, Medicare Part A also partially pays for skilled nursing care. The first 20 days per benefit period are fully paid for by Medicare. Then you split the costs with Medicare up to the hundredth day of your skilled nursing care stay.

You can easily find the exact and specific details of Medicare Part A coverage at medicare.gov.

PART B

Medicare Part B is what most people consider to be "regular" health insurance, and oddly enough, it's an optional coverage. And by "optional," the government means they will penalize you if you don't enroll in it. There are a few exceptions to the rule, but most people are incentivized by a penalty to enroll in Medicare Part B.

You pay a monthly premium for Part B, and it defrays the cost of doctor visits and various other outpatient services. The cost of your monthly premium is based on your modified Adjusted Gross Income (AGI), which is determined during tax filing. Depending on your income, you'll pay somewhere between $100 and $350 monthly for Part B coverage.

Although Part B has a very low deductible that doesn't even exceed $200, it does have a co-pay feature that requires the insured to pay for 20 percent of medical costs once the deductible is met. The 20 percent is paid for either by the insured directly or through a supplemental policy colloquially knows as a *Medigap* policy.

Part B includes X-rays, limited ambulance services, lab and diagnostic testing, vaccinations, and various other services.

PART C (MEDICARE ADVANTAGE)
Medicare Advantage, also known as Part C, is a coverage alternative offered through a network of private insurance companies. Medicare Advantage plans must cover everything that Part B covers but can offer enhanced coverages on top of that, such as lower co-pays and lower out-of-pocket costs. Other optional benefits are prescription coverage and vision and hearing services.

These plans are offered as an alternative to Medigap policies. In fact, if you decide on Medicare Advantage, you are forbidden by law to buy a Medigap policy as well. To get similar benefits to Medicare Advantage, you'd need to sign up for traditional Medicare (Parts A and B), sign up for Part D (prescription coverage), and buy a Medigap policy. This is why so many people choose to simply sign up for Medicare Advantage.

PART D

Simply put, Part D covers prescription drug costs. Alas, if it were only that simple. Part D plans are offered by private healthcare and prescription service groups. They vary in terms of what drugs are covered and to what degree.

Don't assume you don't need Part D if you don't take any prescription drugs. Your health may change, and it can be prudent to have some prescription drug coverage.

The cost for Part D plans varies wildly based on both your income and what type of prescriptions you hope to have covered. Part D is optional.

MEDIGAP

Whether you like it or not, there are several holes in the Medicare system. Even if you have Plans A, B, and D, you still may be exposed to huge out-of-pocket expenses. This is why some people choose to buy supplemental coverage through private insurance companies. These plans are often called *Medigap* coverage.

Medigap coverage can help lessen the costs associated with Parts A and B by helping you pay for the co-insurance (20 percent of costs after the deductible is met).

The introduction of Medicare Advantage has made it tougher to decide whether to buy a Medigap policy. There are advantage and disadvantages to either choice. Start your exploration of how these plans match up with your particular life and health needs at medicare.gov.

MEDICAID

Medicaid is a social healthcare program primarily designed to help the impoverished. And while many mistake Medicaid as a program primarily designed for aging Americans, it is not. Medicaid provides care for low-income individuals and families of all ages, including children. Additionally, Medicaid is the source of care for people on disability.

As it relates to your life in your sixties or older, Medicaid often steps in to assist with the costs associated with long-term care. If you don't have long-term care insurance or money to pay for long-term care expenses, then you may be eligible for Medicaid. To become eligible for Medicaid, you must demonstrate both low income and low assets.

It is not uncommon for individuals to try to circumvent Medicaid rules by transferring money out of their name and title, thus appearing impoverished. Because of this, there is a rule called the *five-year look-back period*. When you apply for Medicaid, the last five years of your finances are scrutinized to determine whether assets were transferred so you could become Medicaid-eligible. If transfers are detected, penalties are assigned that affect the timing of benefit eligibility. In other words, if you have transferred assets out of your name to appear as though you don't have any money, you will have to wait to receive aid.

Trying to circumvent the Medicaid laws is not advisable. Doing so can leave you with no money and no means of medical care.

REVIEW YOUR COVERAGE ANNUALLY

Short of major swings in your investment portfolio, the primary risks you will face over the next several years will all come in the form of healthcare expense risk. If you are not properly covered, you risk spending through your retirement savings and leaving yourself in both a medical and a financial lurch. As you've learned, the Medicare process is a vital piece of your financial pie.

Protect yourself with long-term care insurance and the proper amount of life insurance to ensure that you can enjoy your retirement and not be left worrying about your financial solvency.

CHAPTER 9

THE PLAN

You've no doubt learned a great number of technical processes in this book. But it's the nontechnical lessons that will determine your financial future. These nontechnical lessons are a series of questions you need to answer, more than anything else. It's possible for you to have gotten this far without a plan. But heading into your retirement years without having a plan or having answered some very important questions is a giant mistake.

Before we get to the plan, take a few minutes to consider and honestly address the following questions:

▶ How far removed are you from the worst decade of your financial life? And what has changed since then?

▶ Have your financial habits, in terms of saving and debt reduction, improved substantially in the last five years?

▶ How confident are you that you can retire at your desired retirement age?

▶ Are you ignoring any aspect of your financial life in order to soften the blow of disappointment or worry?

▶ Have you broken your dependence on your income?

With every passing year, the convenient excuses as to why you aren't where you want to be financially seem to disappear. The excuses stop feeling convenient and begin to ring of apathy. At what point is your inaction benign? And at what point is your inaction a dereliction of duty to yourself? Awareness without action is a bad place to be. You must take action.

For every day that you don't address your debt, your debt gets worse. For every day that you don't fund an emergency fund, the greater the impact of small financial emergencies will be. And for every day that you don't save for retirement, the harder saving will become for your future self.

You need a plan. More specifically, you need a plan that takes into account what you've done and what you haven't done. I've found that people often get paralyzed when flooded with the tasks they haven't completed. Creating a plan for your finances sounds much more intimidating than it actually is. Figuring out what to do next needs to be a very simple process. There's only one way to achieve planning simplicity. We're going to harken back to yesteryear and employ the most reader-driven writing technique of all time: the *Choose Your Own Adventure* book.

If you aren't familiar with *Choose Your Own Adventure* books, you're in for a treat. Navigate through the following series of questions. As you answer the questions, jump to the section that applies to your answer. Follow the directions, make choices, follow more directions, and before you know it, you've taken action.

Do not overcomplicate this process. Your focus and action should be singular. Don't just start throwing money at all of your different financial priorities. If everything is a priority, then nothing is a priority. It's easy to get stressed out when you feel the pressure to get so much accomplished all at the same time.

CHOOSE YOUR OWN ADVENTURE

Do not skip ahead. Answer each question and then follow the plan provided.

QUESTIONS

A. Have you started contributing enough to maximize the match offered by your employer-sponsored retirement plan—for example, your 401(k)?

> If yes, go to Question B.

> If no, go to Plan 1.

B. Do you maintain a budget on a monthly basis?

> If yes, go to Question C.

> If no, go to Plan 2.

C. Do you have $1,000 in savings?

> If yes, go to Question D.

> If no, go to Plan 3.

D. Do you have long-term care insurance?

> If yes, go to Question E.

> If no, go to Plan 4.

E. Do you have any credit card debt?

> If yes, go to Plan 5.

> If no, go to Question F.

F. Do you have a fully funded emergency fund (three months of expenses)?

> If yes, go to question G.

> If no, go to Plan 6.

G. Do you have children?

> If yes, go to Question H.

> If no, go to Question J.

H. Do you have any more college funding responsibilities for them?

> If yes, go to Question I.

> If no, go to Plan 7.

I. Do you have parent student loan debt?

> If yes, go to Plan 8.

> If no, go to Question J.

J. Do you plan on increasing the percentage of your income you put toward your retirement plan every year?

> If yes, go to Question K.

> If no, go to Plan 9.

K. Do you have a financial advisor?

> If yes, go to Question L.

> If no, go to Plan 10.

L. Are you maxing out your retirement plans?

> If yes, go to Question M.
>
> If no, go to Plan 11.

M. Are you saving at least 20 percent of your take-home pay?

> If yes, go to Question N.
>
> If no, go to Plan 12.

N. Have you paid off your home?

> If yes, go to Question O.
>
> If no, go to Plan 13.

O. Have you practiced retirement?

> Just go to Plan 14.

PLANS

1. Do it. Talk to your human resources person and ask them the process. You may have to wait for open-enrollment season, or you may be able to fill out the proper paperwork and get started today. Once you've set it up and your first contribution takes place, proceed to Question B.

2. Your focus must instantly turn to resourcefulness. While earning more money may be a solution to some of your financial issues, taking control of your spending will allow you to become efficient and purposeful. Fill out your budget chart and start cutting spending so you can put a focused amount of money toward your

goals on a monthly basis. Once you've captured some money to put toward your goals, proceed to Question C.

3. Saving $1,000 now becomes your primary focus. In fact, you should obsess over it. Work extra hours if possible. Reduce your spending. Your $1,000 starter emergency fund will allow you to address other areas of your financial life without leaving you too vulnerable to life's surprises. Once you've saved $1,000, proceed to Question D.

4. Your decision to address your financial priorities is a noble one, but you risk everything if you don't account for risk. Long-term care insurance protects the assets that you've worked so hard to accumulate. In addition, long-term care insurance allows your significant other to live comfortably, even though you might be in an assisted living facility. Once you've properly addressed your insurance needs, proceed to Question E.

5. Using the momentum method you learned in Chapter 2, create your debt pay-down table and start working it. Eliminate the smallest debt first and keep grinding until your debts are paid off. When people decide to address their debt, it's not uncommon for them to feel like the money that flows toward debt reduction is spent money. Because if the money doesn't go toward fun stuff and the money isn't being saved, then it must be considered spent, right? Well, that's simply not true. Paying off debt has the exact same effect on a person's net worth as saving money does. Once your credit card debts are vanquished, proceed to Question F.

6. A fully funded emergency fund is the closest thing you can be to bulletproof. Your focus can officially turn to wiping out your other debts, saving for a major purchase, and investing for retirement. Once your emergency fund is fully funded, proceed to Question G.

7. You owe it to your children to take the time to decide how their college education will be paid for if they choose to go to college. If you don't take the time to put thought into this decision, the result can be a nasty mix of debt, regret, and a delay in retirement. You cannot just hope that things work out. They won't. If you plan on participating in your child's education expenses, start saving money today. If you need to clean up some debt, that's fine, but just know that the income you've put toward your debt should be reallocated to college saving once the debts are paid off. Proceed to Question I.

8. Parent student loans can destroy your chance at retirement. Do not take them or their payments lightly. Sure, they can hang out in your life for a few more years, but if you've already accomplished all of the other questions and plans before this one, then it's time to be done with parent student loans. Focus all the money you freed up for your financial priorities on paying off your parent student loans. When you've accomplished this, proceed to Question J.

9. Your goals should be to save a higher percentage of your income every year until you retire. If you do this, you will easily be able to transition from your work income to your retirement income. Not only will you have enough money set aside for the future, but you also will be much less dependent on money altogether. Proceed to Question K.

10. A good financial advisor can enhance your financial future. Given that you've made it to this point in your adventure, you will have eliminated your financial past, mastered your financial present, and turned your sights to your financial future. Your financial future is exactly what a good financial advisor specializes in. Set a deadline to interview two or three financial advisors in the next 30 days. Let them know you've cleaned up your debt, have solid spending habits, and are primarily looking for someone to help you harness your income to fund your future. Proceed to Question L.

11. The IRS will actually cut you a break if you let them. By IRS code, you can deduct a significant amount of money from your income if you deposit that money into a qualified retirement fund. Stay current on contribution limits, as they change nearly every year. As you've learned, when you go without that income now, you begin to break your dependency on your work income, which will serve you well in retirement. Proceed to Question M.

12. Do you want to get "in the zone"? Then don't create new financial obligations by taking on debts and new payments. It's not enough to have a significant amount of discretionary income with no true obligations. You must consistently transition this freedom into savings. If you are consistently blowing through your discretionary income, then you are dependent on the income. Once you've begun to save 20 percent of your take-home pay toward nonqualified investments, push yourself further. And now on to Question N.

13. You can take the pressure off of your retirement income by paying off your home as quickly as possible. Once your home is paid off, you will be able to save more money, invest more money, and most importantly, reduce the amount of retirement income you will need to cover your expenses. It's time for Question O.

14. If you haven't retired before, which it's likely you haven't, you need to practice being retired. I know, it sounds strange. But you need to practice living on the income that will be available to you in retirement. You can't expect to magically be given the ability to live on less, once you retire. You have to force the issue. You need to know whether your retirement income streams can support your retirement expenses. This is best accomplished with a practice retirement. I suggest trying to live on your projected retirement income for 90 days. You'll learn a lot about your financial life when you hypothetically remove your work income and start living on your permanent fixed income.

OTHER SOLID GOALS FOR AGE 60

If the preceding plans weren't enough for you, then let's establish a few more reasonable goals to accomplish by age 60.

- ▶ Make maximum annual contributions to your company-sponsored retirement plan.

- ▶ Make maximum annual contributions to a Health Savings Account, if applicable.

- ▶ Establish permanent financial independence from both your parents and your children via proper planning.

- ▶ Complete a comprehensive estate plan with an estate-planning attorney.

- ▶ Create a thorough retirement plan, in terms of how you will spend your time in retirement. It's not a 1,000-week vacation. It's a significant period of your life.

BE CAREFUL OF DOLLAR GOALS

You'll notice that I'm not too interested in establishing a dollar-amount goal for you. There are several reasons for this, but the most important reason is that your resourcefulness is just as important as your resources. Millions of dollars of retirement money can be mishandled, whether you believe it or not.

I once witnessed a 59-year-old couple blow through 12 percent of their retirement assets in their first year of retirement, 14 percent in their second year of retirement, and 13 percent in their third year of retirement. They certainly have several issues, but I always thought their primary issue was their two-decade obsession with saving $1 million for retirement. Upon reaching their $1 million goal, which was primarily funded by the sale of a business, they retired, and things started to unravel.

I've seen couples have their retirement funded by an inheritance and go off the rails just the same. Large influxes of money into a retirement plan can create major problems if resourcefulness isn't part of the mix.

Remember, resourcefulness can bring resources, but resources cannot bring resourcefulness.

YOUR DILIGENCE AND DISCIPLINE WILL PAY DIVIDENDS

I'm not asking that you spend hours per month dealing with your financial life. In fact, I'm asking that you dedicate around 30 minutes per month to make sure you don't have to spend hours per month worrying about your financial life. Every month you should run through your budget, check on your debt-repayment schedule, and then reconfirm your current singular objective.

You will be faced with the temptations of convenience, apathy, and ignorance. But none of those things will give you the sort of financial life you really want.

Don't ignore your financial past. Be wise in the present. And prepare for your future. It's *Your Money Life.*

INDEX

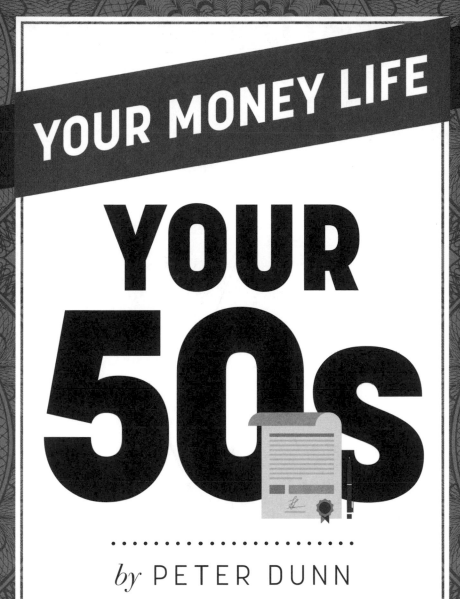

YOUR MONEY LIFE

YOUR 50s

by PETER DUNN

Pete*the*Planner

PETE*the*PLANNER.com

The PATH

Your fifties could easily be the best decade of your life. In this decade you are in your prime earning years, your commitments to your children are lessening, and you are getting closer and closer to retirement. But, the excitement of this decade can also be what derails your plans. Becoming overconfident, or worse, overspending, can delay retirement. There are a few roadblocks to watch out for as you head into your sixties. Fill out this quiz to see what areas you need to watch out for.

1. Do you currently provide financial assistance of any type to your adult children or grandchildren?
2. If so, how much money do you spend per month on assistance?
3. Did you pay for your children's education?
4. Do you have any student loan obligations resulting from your children's education?
5. Have you cosigned on any other type of loan for your children?
6. Do you currently provide financial assistance of any type to your parents or grandparents?
7. If so, how much money do you spend per month on assistance?

To be able to exit your fifties with ease, you'll need to focus on correcting a few bumps in the road. Don't let these bumps become major roadblocks to retirement in your sixties; make the effort now to get on the right track.

CHILDREN

As a parent, your role from the very beginning is to step in and fix problems, no matter how ridiculous. (I'm looking at you toddler years.) As your kids grow older, you might be able to work in a moral lesson, but you are still there to solve the problem. This is a very hard habit to break. So hard, in fact, that most parents just don't. Your adult child's financial problems are not your financial problems. Think of it this way: If you don't cut off your kids now, it impedes your ability to retire, which means that in 20 years when you run out of money, you're going to have to rely on your kids for support. Break the cycle now.

PARENTS

Speaking of cycles, you may also be caring for aging parents. Whether it is out of the goodness of your heart or it's necessary for their well-being you may be financially supporting your parents. It's time to have an open and honest conversation with your parents. What does their financial future look like? What is your role? Will this conversation be awkward? Absolutely. But it's also absolutely necessary.

The PAST

List your debts, beginning with the debt that has the smallest balance and working your way up to the highest balance debt. Be sure to include all debts; to help jog your memory see pages 21–37 for a full list of types of debt.

DEBT	BALANCE	MINIMUM PAYMENT	MONTHLY PAYMENT
TOTALS			

The **PRESENT**

SPENDING

Find money today by working through this list of services you use. Can you decrease your usage? Or switch to a cheaper plan? Decreasing expenses starts here!

EXPENSE	CURRENT PAYMENT	ROOM FOR IMPROVEMENT?	SAVINGS AMOUNT
INTERNET			
CABLE			
HOME PHONE			
CELL PHONE			
MOVIE SUBSCRIPTION			
MUSIC SUBSCRIPTION			
TOTALS			

The PIE

BUDGETING

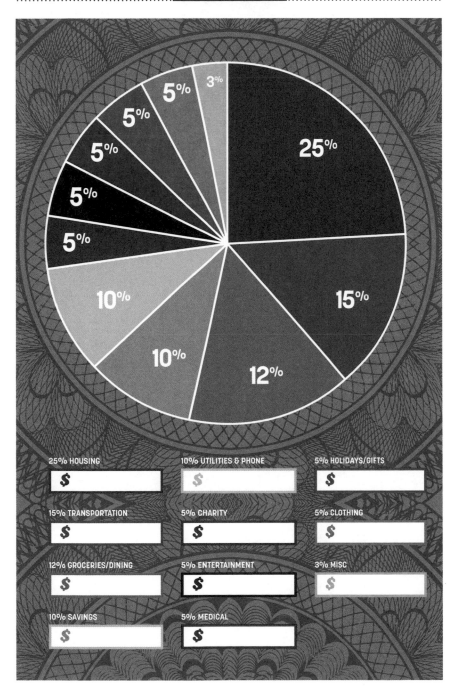

25%

15%

12%

10%

10%

5%

5%

5%

5%

5%

3%

25% HOUSING
$

10% UTILITIES & PHONE
$

5% HOLIDAYS/GIFTS
$

15% TRANSPORTATION
$

5% CHARITY
$

5% CLOTHING
$

12% GROCERIES/DINING
$

5% ENTERTAINMENT
$

3% MISC
$

10% SAVINGS
$

5% MEDICAL
$

The PIE

YOUR MONTHLY HOUSEHOLD INCOME $

HOUSING   **TRANSPORTATION**

HOUSING		TRANSPORTATION	
Mortgage/Rent		Car Payment A	
Electric		Car Payment B	
Gas		Gasoline	
Phone		Maintenance	
Cell		Auto Insurance	
Cable		License Plates	
Internet		Total	
Water			
Waste		**FOOD**	
Lawn Care		Groceries	
HOA		Coffee	
Other		Work Lunch	
Total		Dining Out	
		Total	

BUDGETING CONT.

PERSONAL CARE		EXISTING DEBT	
		(CREDIT CARDS, STUDENT LOANS) NOT CARS	
Clothing		Debt Payment #1	
Cleaning/Laundry		Debt Payment #2	
Hair Care		Debt Payment #3	
Medical		Debt Payment #4	
Books/Subscriptions		Debt Payment #5	
Entertainment		Debt Payment #6	
Gifts		Debt Payment #7	
Pets		Debt Payment #8	
Total		Total	

SAVINGS AND INSURANCE	
Savings	
Life Insurance	
IRA/Roth IRA	
College Savings	
Total	

TOTAL

The POSSESSIONS

This decade of your life, your fifties, can bring significant expenses associated with big purchases. Sure, there are the major purchases you're used to, like a house and a car. But your fifties may have also brought events like college educations and weddings. Your fifties can cost you a lot of money. Work through the following sections to determine spending and to find ways to improve your situation.

HOUSE

Current or projected monthly mortgage payment: **$**
Current monthly income: **$**
Divide the top number by the bottom number to get the percentage of take-home pay you are spending on housing expenses: **$**

* 40 PERCENT OR MORE OF HOUSEHOLD INCOME COMMITTED TO HOUSING. Your margin of error is very slim. You are clinically overhoused. You should seek an immediate solution to this problem, especially if you have a car payment, student loan debt, and/or other consumer debt.

* 26 TO 39 PERCENT OF HOUSEHOLD INCOME COMMITTED TO HOUSING. You listened to the bank, or you followed the advice of a mortgage calculator. You are spending too much on housing, but it's not a fatal error. But if you have a car payment or debt, then you are at risk of hating your financial life for a long time.

* 25 PERCENT OF HOUSEHOLD INCOME COMMITTED TO HOUSING. Life is manageable, fruitful, and comfortable when you can limit your house payment to 25 percent of your income. You can get the best of both worlds: a nice home and a nice payment.

* LESS THAN 25 PERCENT OF HOUSEHOLD INCOME COMMITTED TO HOUSING. Do you want everything and are willing to sacrifice a foolish housing decision to get it? Awesome. Then spend less than 25 percent of your household income on a house payment. Travel the world. Dine out. Drive a sweet ride. You can do these things when you don't over-commit to ridiculous housing costs.

Homeowners, also beware of the costly home improvement project! A Home Equity Line of Credit (HELOC) is tempting to tap into, but don't forget, it's debt. The better alternative is to bust your hump and save for the project. Your basement remodel is going to cost $10,000? Cool. *Start saving.*

VEHICLE

HERE'S YOUR VEHICLE SPENDING GUIDE:
What is your net monthly household income? **$**

What is 15% of your net monthly household income? **$**

How do your current transportation costs compare to this number? Let's take a look, starting with monthly costs.

Current car payment: **$**

Current monthly fuel cost: **$**

Current monthly insurance cost: **$**

Total monthly costs: **$**

DON'T FORGET TO FACTOR IN ANNUAL COSTS!

Maintenance: **$**

Oil-change costs: **$**

Tires: **$**

Car washes: **$**

Repairs: **$**

Total maintenance: **$**

Monthly maintenance
(the total above, divided by 12): **$**

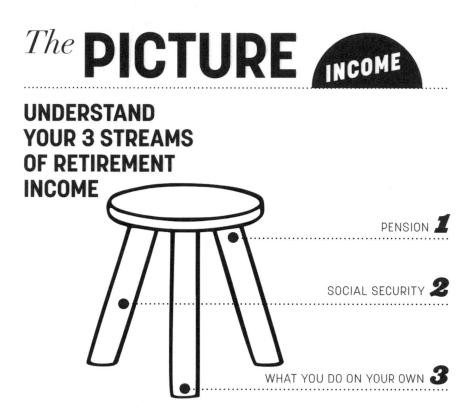

The PICTURE INCOME

UNDERSTAND YOUR 3 STREAMS OF RETIREMENT INCOME

PENSION **1**

SOCIAL SECURITY **2**

WHAT YOU DO ON YOUR OWN **3**

Project your income at retirement by putting your numbers into the calculator at *PeteThePlanner.com/retirement-calculator*.

Once you have your projected retirement income, go back to the Monte Carlo simulation tables on pages 168–170. Find the table that most closely matches your projected investment style and philosophy. Next, choose a distribution rate for your income-producing assets. Four percent is the best distribution rate to shoot for.

YOUR PROCESS MIGHT LOOK LIKE THIS:

1. Determine that your $400,000 portfolio will grow to $600,000 over the next 10 years, given a particular rate of return and the proper additions.

2. Select the Monte Carlo simulation table created using a 60 percent stock and 40 percent bond allocation, if it is indeed your investment style and mix.

3. Select a distribution rate of 4 percent.

4. Confirm that you are comfortable that a 4 percent distribution rate has a 92 percent chance for success over 30 years of distributions.

The PIGGY BANK

WHAT'S IN MY BUCKETS

You have three buckets of money.
Well, you SHOULD have three buckets of money.
It's okay if you don't; we'll help you with that.
These buckets of money will be all you need
to help you along your financial journey.

$ | $ | $

SHORT-TERM

Bucket #1 is your short-term savings. It consists of three months' worth of your household expenses. When this bucket has three months' worth of expenses, stop putting money in it. If you need money for an emergency, then take the money from this bucket. It is your permanent emergency fund.

MID-TERM

Bucket #2 is your mid-term savings. This consists of down payment money, college funds, and any other amount of money that isn't specifically dedicated to your emergency fund (Bucket #1) or retirement (Bucket #3). You may choose to simply save this money, or you may choose to invest this money. Whatever you choose, make sure you talk to a professional before you take undue risk.

LONG-TERM

Bucket #3 is your long-term savings. You commonly refer to this as your retirement money. Technically speaking, you can't touch this money until you are 59 ½ years old. Is that a ridiculously random age? Yes. Are you in trouble if you don't have any money in Bucket #3? Absolutely. You should start contributing to Bucket #3 as soon as you get a job. Contribute to your retirement account through your employer at least up to what the employer matches.

GO TO **PETETHEPLANNER.COM/RETIREMENT-CALCULATOR**
TO CALCULATE HOW MUCH YOU NEED TO SAVE FOR RETIREMENT.

CALCULATE YOUR NET WORTH

WHAT'S YOUR ASSET TOTAL?

We calculated your total debt earlier. Write that debt total below.

WHAT'S YOUR DEBT TOTAL?

Subtract the debt from the assets. This is your net worth. It may be positive. It may be negative. Your goal is to make it go in the right direction. You can do this by paying down debt. You can do this by saving money. Or you can do this by doing both. *Do both.*

NET WORTH

The PITFALLS

You have purchased several types of insurance in your lifetime. In fact, you've probably bought a combination of life, disability, health, car, homeowners, and some other form of insurance. That's a lot of premiums. Your insurance needs will continue to evolve throughout your life. As you progress through your fifties and into your sixties, your insurance needs will change.

USE THE CHART BELOW TO DETERMINE WHAT INSURANCES YOU NEED TO KEEP AND WHAT POLICIES YOU CAN CHANGE OR EVEN LET GO OF.

TYPE OF INSURANCE	COVERAGE IMPROVEMENT?	MONTHLY PREMIUM	ROOM FOR IMPROVEMENT?
HEALTH			
CAR			
RENTERS			
HOMEOWNERS			
LIFE			
DISABILITY			

THE PLAN

Your fifties can be an amazing decade.
They can be one of freeing financial security and endless opportunities. This also leaves you open to complacency and mistakes. Don't risk your future by making blunders this late in the game.

IN THIS DECADE WATCH OUT FOR THE FOLLOWING FINANCIAL TRAPS:

- Taking on a new mortgage that you won't be able to pay off by retirement
- Continuing to offer financial assistance to adult children
- Offering financial assistance to parents without a plan
- Accruing consumer debt

HOPEFULLY, YOU DID ALL THE HARD WORK IN YOUR TWENTIES, THIRTIES, AND FORTIES AND YOU'LL NOW BE ABLE TO REAP THOSE REWARDS IN THIS DECADE. TO CONTINUE YOUR GREAT TRAJECTORY, WORK ON THESE GOALS HEADING INTO YOUR SIXTIES:

- Make maximum annual contributions to your company-sponsored retirement plan.
- Make maximum annual contributions to a Health Savings Account, if applicable.
- Purchase long-term care insurance.
- Establish permanent financial independence from both your parents and your children, via proper planning.
- Hire a financial advisor.
- Make a plan to have your mortgage, as well as any other debt, paid off before retirement.
- Complete a comprehensive estate plan with an estate-planning attorney.
- Project income forward into retirement and practice living on that amount now.
- Create a thorough retirement plan, in terms of how you will spend your time in retirement. It's not a 1,000-week vacation. *It's a significant period of your life.*